To Joe-Joe-San

from

Char-And-Fran

Translators note:

.If you need to order any special
ingredients. please inform dishonorable
friends Framank Char & they will send to you
at no special cost - heart's love is only fee for service

JAPANESE FOOD AND COOKING

Japanese Food and Cooking

by Stuart Griffin

CHARLES E. TUTTLE COMPANY

Rutland, Vermont　　　　　Tokyo, Japan

Published by Charles E. Tuttle Co.
of Rutland, Vermont & Tokyo, Japan
with editorial offices at
15 Edogawa-cho, Bunkyo-ku, Tokyo

Library of Congress Catalog
Card No. 55-10617

First printing, April 1956
Eighth printing, 1961

Printed in Japan

CONTENTS

14. Desserts .... ,................. 140

15. Festival Dishes 152

16. Table Utensils 159

17. Table Manners 162

FOREWORD

Before Mrs. American Housewife docked at Yokohama or landed at Haneda, her husband Mr. American had scoured the Japanese scene, gastronomically.

Mr. American Husband—sergeant, captain, civilian, diplomat, businessman, correspondent, missionary, tourist, teacher, or student—had really looked around, seeking occasional relief from his dearly beloved steak and French fries, or ham and eggs, in the sizzling meat and vegetables of *sukiyaki*, the hot, chewy custard of *chawan mushi*, or the brown crispness of *tempura*.

Mr. American Husband, civilian or military, had strolled from the broad avenues and wandered into the back kitchens around Shimbashi and Shinjuku, behind the Ginza, ea and west. There, in the midst of steam and noise, he had followed his happy nostrils in the general direction of what his stomach liked and what his wallet could afford.

He tracked down *yakitori*, or roasted chicken on

spits ; uncoiled and dripped throat-ward chilled or steamed noodles ; chopsticked *kabayaki*, or broiled split eels on rice ; sucked up *misoshiru*, or bean-paste soup ; speared *kamaboko*, or fish gelatine; and even chewed and swallowed *sashimi*, or raw fish.

He found what he liked, and what he didn't like.

Defiantly, he could walk past the big, briny tubs of pickles, the fish stands where every species eyed him, and the small stool-and-counter shops with the stomach-turning cooking-oil smells. Mr. American Husband could leave a lot of Japanese food alone. He guessed he'd have to be reborn to sniff, let alone swallow some of what he saw. But he found lots of things that he wanted to eat and did like.

Perhaps his major discovery was how good fish could be. This and other information he filed away. Then he went to greet Mrs. American Housewife.

She arrives. All is strange, hard to understand. The food—she never gives it a thought. The maid knows her way around a lamb chop; can mash potatoes with the best ; serves " sunny-side-up " eggs; perks coffee ; and handles in stride tossed salads, pancakes, hominy, cheese soufflé, and shepherd's pie.

Mrs. American Housewife unpacks skillets, chafing dishes, and cookie moulds ; unwraps her glassware from excelsior. The rest is up to Michiko or Yoshie under Mrs. Housewife's eyes, and in English.

The first break with convention : eating rice.

Yoshie or Michiko slaps down a big white mound besides the peas and carrots, in the home-fry's shadow, next to bread and butter. "Starch!" gasps Mrs. American Housewife in a stricken voice, but yields.

Rice is tasty. The conspiracy begins to pay off. American Husband and Japanese Maid exchange glances. Wife likes rice—*Ah so!* Wife laughs; says she has never eaten rice since her mother scolded and said, "Now, eat your rice pudding, or else!"

Husband watches with interest. Then he speaks tentatively.

"We should go out to dinner some night."

This he handles carefully. Wife, gastronomically, is entrenched behind the Maginot Line of canned soup, liver and bacon, Waldorf salad, pie à la mode, and demitasse. She mustn't suspect.

But they go out to dinner. She thinks of course he means the Imperial, the Tokyo Kaikan, or some place with French, German, or Italian cooking. Japanese— the last thought in her mind.

She supposes the Japanese eat— and she lets it go at that. "Fish heads and rice?" Yes, probably.

"Yes," she replies, "let's go eat outside. It'll be fun." This line is her downfall.

The day of the great test dawns clear and cold— soon, it's evening. Husband has masterminded his plans all day. What they eat, or don't, will make him or break him.

The Chinese say that the journey of a thousand miles begins with but a single step. What is that step?

There is only one answer: *Sukiyaki.*

And Wife is wild about it.

Husband knows victory's sweet flavor when Wife sinks against the wall, eyes half shut, bliss itself.

"My, that was delicious. I could almost eat another panful!"

Later, they have a party. It gets late; the guests go home. It has been a brilliantly successful dinner party. Everyone liked what they ate, few knowing what they ate. The dinner was entirely Japanese.

Husband still hears the "thank you" compliments; still sees Wife beaming at the doorstep.

"...What was that soup called? Maybe your Michiko could teach my Sumie."

"...Delightful, wonderful. What was in it?"

"...George and I were just saying how we'd love to serve such a dinner."

"You can," says Husband, "you can indeed." He feels the crusader spirit, the nobility of helping one's fellowman. He shares this impulse with Wife, now almost as "bamboo" as he.

"Say," he calls out, "we should knock out a few pages on our favorite Japanese dishes. Just something simple that everyone could follow. Help a lot of people that way, we could!"

Wife caught Husband's enthusiasm.

"Swell idea," she said, "let's do it, honey."

Which could just as easily have been the way this little cookbook started.

INGREDIENTS

There is scarcely a foreigner who, having enjoyed the wide range of Japanese foods, hasn't marveled at the richly assorted ingredients that go into these dishes, seventy-five at least that are distinct and individual, perhaps more.

One should first know what is at hand, at the "culinary command"; what can be bought in the way of meats, fish, vegetables, sauces, specialties, fruits, and the like.

And then one can proceed to prepare, as this little recipe book suggests, some of the many tasty dishes foreigners will always love.

Meat is available in all forms: beef, pork, veal, lamb, and the subdivisions of chops, bacon, liver, sweetbreads, kidneys, etc. Poultry and game are just as easy to find: chicken, turkey, goose, duck, capon, rabbit, pheasant, partridge, wild boar, deer, quail, etc.

Foreigners may wince at first reading of the following paragraphs, but this is a mistake, correctible in the eating. And the eating of course is in the cooking.

Available fish include: seabream, bonito, salmon, cod, sardines, flounder, tuna, mackerel, trout, herring, shark, whale, eel, red snapper, and many others. Kindred marine life includes : prawns, shrimp, crab, squid, cuttlefish, oysters, blowfish, abalone, scallops, clams, and edible seaweed.

Vegetables are equally abundant: beans, cucumbers, corn, peas, leeks, onions, pumpkin, sprouts, cabbage, tomatoes, lettuce, carrots, turnips, squash, spinach, radishes, parsley, celery, beets, mushrooms, and at a few fancier places, lima beans, okra, asparagus, broccoli, green peppers, rhubarb, and the like.

There are many distinctive Japanese vegetables: *gobo*, or burdock; *negi*, or leeks; *daikon*, or white radish; *takenoko*, or bamboo sprouts; *seri*, or Japanese parsley; *renkon*, or lotus; *mitsuba*, or marsh parsley; *konnyaku*, or root paste; *wasabi*, or horseradish; *moyashi*, or bean sprouts; *shoga*, or ginger; *ginnan*, or gingko nuts; *nasu*, or eggplant; *kikutane*, or chrysanthemum seeds; *shitake*, or tree mushrooms ; and such local mushroom varieties as *hatsudake*, *shoro*, *shimeji*, and *kotake*.

Also easily available are such vegetable by-products as *shirataki*, or devilsfoot noodles ; *soba*, or buckwheat

2

noodles ; *fu*, or wheat gluten; *tofu*, or bean curd; *yuba*, or dried bean curd ; and *udon*, or macaroni.

There are also many kinds of fruit: apples, peaches, plums, pears, melons, grapes, cherries, loquats, lemons, oranges, grapefruits, persimmons, and berries. Cross-breeding has evolved the *natsumikan*, or summer mandarin; *nijuseki*, or pear-apples ; and others. Bananas and pineapple are available, also dates, figs, raisins, etc.

There is variety among the appetizers. Before a meal or with tea, one may eat small egg-rolls; fried egg-yolk squares; hot, steamed, sugared red beans; mullet roe; quail eggs; fish-paste squares; bean-filled rice or wheat buns; rice or wheat wafers; bean-paste squares and jellies; seaweed rice-cakes, painted with *shoyu* sauce; and wafers. One may have boiled-down sweetened agar-agar, millet-jelly sweets, or hard rice biscuits. The appetizers in fact often overlap into desserts, as indeed do the fruits.

Spices, sauces, and flavorings are most important to Japanese cooking. Foremost of these is *shoyu*, or soy sauce, made from wheat or barley, soybeans, salt, and water. A dark, inky, thirst-provoking liquid, it is similar to that found in Chinese restaurants.

The wheat is grilled in a big iron pan until burnt-brown in hue. It is then crushed. Beans are boiled in an adjacent cauldron, with a heavy weight on the lid. Boiling lasts three to five hours, then the fire is put out, and the beans are kept in the kettle overnight. Steaming may be used as a method of bean preparation. This process lasts for five or six hours.

The grilled wheat and boiled beans are mixed and placed in a malt-room where malt seed are added. The mixture turns to malt in a few days. Salt water is put over the malt and left for a few more days, being stirred occasionally until fermentation takes place.

This over-all mixture is pressed, and the sauce obtained is bottled.

Miso is another necessity. This is a mixture of malt, salt, and mashed soybeans, the liquor of which is drained off in tubs and allowed to ferment. *Miso* will be discussed later, in the soup chapter.

Dashi is another favorite seasoning. It comes from two chief ingredients: *kombu*, or tangle, and *katsuobushi*, or dried bonito. The bones are extracted, and the fish is dried in ovens. The green mildew that is residual from the drying improves the flavor.

The finished product is shaved and used for over-all flavoring. *Dashi* itself is a clear liquid, used as soup stock or foundation. In its place, or as an additional ingredient, *Aji-no-Moto*, a Japanese seasoning, may be used. This is a recipe that will be used throughout this cookbook, as *dashi* is a basic stock for the preparation of most Japanese foods.

Katsuobushi is first shaved, more easily if it has been warmed over a fire first; for one serving, one tablespoon of this dried fish is used. *Kombu* is the other chief ingredient in making *dashi*. It is sliced into small bits.

One should learn carefully how to make *dashi*. The following recipe should make four cups :

Ingredients: ½ cup of *katsuobushi* shavings
¾ square inch tangle
⅛ teaspoon *Aji-no-Moto*, or similar seasoning
4⅓ cups water

Preparation: Place the tangle in water and take out when the water starts to boil. Put the shaved *katsuobushi* into the water and again take out when the water boils. The clear liquid left is *dashi*.

This is a simple recipe but it is one of the most important in Japanese cookery.

Niboshi, a small dry fish, may be boiled with the particular food in place of the *dashi*.

Ground walnuts, sesame seed, *shiso* leaves and berries, red peppers, horseradish, hot mustard, ginger, small tart onions, and peanuts may also be used for flavoring. Vinegar and sugar play key roles.

Wine flavoring too is popular, using *sake*, or rice wine ; or flavored *sake*, called *mirin* or *toso*.

Another spice, a kind of native pepper, is called *sansho*. There is also a citrus called *yuzu*.

A few words of importance to the housewife in respect to sauces and spices seem necessary here :

In general, under the heading Ingredients in each recipe, mention is made of the type of sauce or seasoning required and in what amount. In general, under this heading, directions as to use are not included.

How these sauce-ingredients are employed is detailed in the paragraphs on preparation, immediately following.

In a few cases, easily recognizable, a spice or sauce is used in the preparation of several main items of the recipe. For example, some salt may be used with fish, more salt with vegetables, and still more in the sauce. In such cases, the amount listed refers specifically to the major ingredient and follows directly after it in the ingredient-listing.

Whenever the chief ingredients of a sauce are

brought into the text, it is to be understood that they are added in order, *not* mingled together at the same time. For example, salt is followed by sugar, followed by *shoyu*, and in the specified amounts.

Bear one thing in mind—*each recipe, soon to follow, will be for four persons.*

2
RICE DISHES

It goes without saying that the keynote word for Japanese food and Japanese cooking is rice. It is the staple of the diet of eight-five million inhabitants and increasingly one of the staples of the diet of foreign guests in Japan.

Rice is eaten plain, hot or cold, white and fluffy. It also is eaten soaked in Japanese tea, in a style known as *chazuke*. Rice is the base for a wide variety of Japanese dishes, recipes of which will follow in due course. It is also the basis for many cakes and sweets, and for the national drink, *sake*.

Rice dishes employ fish, eels, meats, fowl, vegetables, and sauces. Some of these dishes are as famous as *sukiyaki* and *tempura*. Others remain to be discovered as this volume proceeds.

The preparation of the rice itself is highly important.

The grains or kernels should be carefully washed

free of all grit and impurities, then put into a special pot that the Japanese call *kama*. Water is added.

According to the consistency of rice desired, the amount of water used will differ. The standard used by the majority of Japanese is 1 cup of rice to $1\frac{1}{4}$ cups of water. The Japanese, in determining the amount of water, spread the rice evenly over the bottom of the *kama* and then add water until the water-level is between $1\frac{1}{4}$ and $1\frac{1}{2}$ inches above the rice-level.

The *kama* is set on a stove or *hibachi* and watched carefully during the cooking. American housewives often prefer the more familiar double boiler.

The watered rice should be boiled thoroughly over a fire strong enough to cause seething, after which the flames are turned low for 10 to 15 minutes to reduce the boiling and keep the bubbling water from escaping over the sides of the cooking vessel.

After this the fire should be turned down still lower for another 10 minute period, after which the flames should be extinguished entirely. The cooked rice is allowed to stand, lid on pot, for another 10 to 15 minutes. This will prevent sticky or gummy rice and will ensure the best-flavored result.

Now we may turn to the first of our recipes, those

in the rice-dish classification. The three chief dishes combine rice with (1) lobster, shrimp, or prawn, (2) eels and (3) chicken and eggs. These and other rice dishes the Japanese call *meshimono*, or literally, rice foods.

Tendon

This recipe is for crustaceans cooked in deep-fat or *tempura* style and served in a bowl on top of white rice.

Ingredients: 14 to 16 ounces lobster, shrimp, or prawns, cooked as described below

4 ounces watercress or thinly sliced carrots

1 cup *dashi*

2 tablespoons sugar

4 tablespoons *shoyu*

4 cups rice

Preparation: The lobster, shrimp, or prawns should be prepared in *tempura* style, which must be described at some length.

Tempura, first of all, is a word with an odd meaning. It is derived from three Japanese ideographs : *tem*

or *ten*, meaning heaven; *pu* or *fu*, meaning woman; and *ra*, meaning silk gauze. It takes perhaps a stretch of the Occidental imagination to see how such a strange and delicious repast can come from such seemingly ill-mated ideographs, but that's the meaning.

Tempura is fried food—dipped in a mixture of egg, water, and flour and fried in oil. Harmony, which is required, is assured by the four elements present : fresh ingredients, a lightly-fried coating, sweet-smelling fresh cooking oils, and a well-prepared sauce.

The *tempura* treatment lends itself equally well to flatfish or white fish; certain vegetables such as leeks, spinach, carrots, and even mushrooms; and other Japanese special vegetables such as burdock, eggplant, sweet onions, and *shungiku*, a fragrant green plant.

To prepare the *tempura* coating mix one full cup of flour with one egg and one cup of water, lightly mixing all three together.

The oil is of great importance. Vegetable oil is used—rice oil, salad oil, sesame seed oil, rapeseed oil, peanut oil, soybean oil, or any others locally available.

One must see that the temperature of the oil is kept between 300 and 350 degrees F. The oil should be about two inches deep.

Sauce, as always, is a top ingredient. For *tempura*

use a boiled mixture of *dashi* (16 tablespoons for 4 people) or fish soup made by boiling the head and bones of a fish. In addition, the mixture must have four tablespoons of *shoyu* and four more of *sake*, or dry cooking sherry.

First, the head, outer hard shell, and inner entrails of the lobster are carefully removed, the tail being left intact. A sharp knife is used to cut lengthwise down the spinal column, taking care not to cut through entirely. Three crosswise cuts are also made, again not all the way through. Shrimp and prawns are similarly cleaned before being used.

Lightly mix the flour, egg, and water; then dip the lobster chunks in the thickened mixture. The lobster should next be inserted slowly into the boiling oil, heated to an even 300 degrees F.

When these pieces have been fried, they are removed, golden and crisp and put on brown paper while the oil drains off.

In the meantime the *dashi* has been boiled with the *shoyu* and the *sake*, and the resultant sauce allowed to cool.

The still-hot lobster is placed on top of the gleaming mound of rice and over all is poured, for extra flavor, the sauce composed of the *dashi-shoyu-sake*, mixed with 4 ounces of grated white radish and a sprinkling of grated ginger. The *tendon* is served individually in a large bowl called a *domburi*.

Vegetables are often added to the *tendon* preparation. The vegetables are cut thin and dipped in the *tempura* batter, just as were the lobster chunks. Then the vegetables are likewise fried in the hot cooking oil. When vegetables are used, the sauce is made of *dashi*, *shoyu*, and sugar.

A word on a possible rice substitute: *udon*, Japanese macaroni, or *soba*, Japanese buckwheat noodles, may be used instead.

Unagi Domburi

Second only to *tendon* among the *meshimono* is this Japanese way of preparing broiled eels and white rice.

Ingredients: 18 ounces fresh live eels
A soup stock made from boiling eels' heads and bones
4 tablespoons *mirin* and 3 tablespoons *shoyu* together
4 cups rice

Preparation: The broiled eels (split

apart with bones removed, skewered and grilled) are placed on top of the rice, inside a red or black lacquerware box. The heated soup stock, made from the eels' heads and bones, and the mixture of *mirin* and *shoyu* is then poured over everything.

Oyako Domburi

Even more delicious, for those who have a natural predisposition to chicken rather than eel, is this dish.

Ingredients: ¹/₄ pound chicken
¹/₄ pound mushrooms
2 onions
4 eggs
Sauce from ¹/₂ cup *dashi*,
   4 tablespoons *shoyu*,
   4 tablespoons *sake*
4 cups rice

Preparation: First, the chicken meat, mushrooms, and onions are sliced thin. Next, the *sake*, *dashi*, and *shoyu* are boiled; when this mixture has come to a boil, the chicken, mushrooms and onions are added and cooked.

One serving of the cooked mixture is placed in a frying pan, and an egg which has been beaten lightly is added. This is allowed to cook, with a minimum of stirring, until almost firm. Remove and serve on top of rice.

The remaining portions are prepared in the same manner. Using the ingredients listed in this recipe four people may be served.

Chicken Rice

This is as simple a recipe as this book contains. But it is appetizing and it is easy to prepare.

Ingredients: 3½ cups rice

4 cups soup made from chicken bones, giblets, and entrails

6 ounces chicken meat

A sauce prepared from 3½ tablespoons *shoyu* and 2 tablespoons *mirin*

1½ sheets seasoned laver

Preparation: The chicken is sliced and steeped in the *shoyu-mirin* sauce for 15 to 20 minutes. Remove the chicken, mix the sauce with the chicken soup which has been prepared from chicken bones, giblets, and entrails.

This mixture is used in lieu of water in boiling the rice. Water may be added to thin the mixture.

The rice is then served in bowls with the chicken slices placed on top of the rice.

This may also be served sprinkled with some crushed *laver*, a kind of seaweed, for extra flavor.

Fish Rice

This dish usually requires the costly sea-bream, or *tai*, but other white-flesh fish may be used.

Ingredients: 3½ cups rice
¾ pound white-flesh fish
4 cups water
4 tablespoons *sake*
1¼ tablespoons salt
1 leek
1½ cups *dashi*
2 dried mushrooms
Some parsley or spinach
A sauce made from ¼ teaspoon *shoyu*, ¼ teaspoon salt, and perhaps some powdered laver

Preparation: The fish is sliced into three chunks. The flesh, head, and bones are boiled in 4 cups of water. The softened flesh is easily removed and should be torn into small pieces, using the fingers. The fish soup is strained free of particles, flavored with *sake* and salt, and then poured, in its entirety, over the rice.

The rice is brought to a slow boil and when it begins to bubble over, the flesh of the fish is added. The rice is then cooked in the standard way.

Stems removed, tough outer skin stripped off, the mushrooms are first softened in tepid water and then, with parsley or spinach (leaves) added, are boiled.

These prepared vegetables are put into the *dashi* and flavored with *shoyu* and salt in the stated amounts.

The rice should always be served in big bowls with the soup poured over. The leek, boiled separately, is chopped up finely, and sprinkled over the rice-soup mixture. The laver may be powdered and added.

Red Rice

Japanese love this dish. To foreigners, it presents a bit of an acquired taste problem, but it has its disciples.

Ingredients: 3½ cups *mochigome* (glutinous rice)

½ cup *azuki* (Japanese beans)

5 cups water

½ tablespoon salt

A mixture of 2 tablespoons black sesame seeds and ½ teaspoon water

Preparation: Rice should be thoroughly washed and rinsed, then left in a basket. Red beans are then boiled in 5 cups of water. They must be constantly stirred.

Cook the rice in the usual way, adding one-half teaspoon of salt and using the reddish water that the beans were boiled in. You may find the residue left from the beans insufficient to cook the rice. Add, if necessary, clear water. After the rice has reached its first boil, add the cooked beans.

The rice and beans are served cold with parched black sesame seeds and a pinch of salt sprinkled over each serving.

Chestnut Rice

Here is an unusual way of presenting an old American favorite—the chestnut.

Ingredients: 3½ cups rice
24 chestnuts
2 tablespoons *shoyu*
½ teaspoon salt
1¼ teaspoons *sake*
4 cups water

Preparation: Chestnuts must first be husked, then halved and allowed to soak and soften in warm water. Rice, as always, is carefully washed before cooking.

Put the rice, flavoring, chestnuts, and water into the *kama*. Set the *kama* on the stove and boil the rice over a very high flame. When the rice boils over, turn the flame low for 20 minutes.

Rice should be allowed to stand for 10 minutes and then be served.

3
RICE-SANDWICHES

Winter or summer, boiling hot or served cold, the culinary emphasis in Japan is always on rice. We have seen how it can be mixed with various kinds of seafoods, vegetables, chicken, and eel to make some of Japan's most notable dishes. Some form of rice is indispensible to any traditional Japanese meal.

And now in *sushi*, the cold but tasty "rice-sandwich," we find another delicious if strange application to which Japan's food staple can be put, a great favorite with many "old Japan hands."

One of the nation's most noted dishes, *sushi* are simply vinegared rice-balls, rolled around or topped with a wide variety of ingredients. *Sushi* might be likened to *hors d'oeuvres* in that they could easily be served as appetizers, although, for the Japanese, *sushi* constitute the entire meal.

Again, the success of the dish lies in the preparation of the rice.

Ingredients: Hard, white polished rice
(in whatever amount desired)

Water (1¼ th of the total rice used)

Vinegar (amount to be explained below)

Sugar and salt

The vinegar required for rice-mixing is broken down as follows: (A) for 5 cups rice, ¾ cups vinegar and 1½ tablespoons salt, and (B) for 5 cups rice, ½ cup vinegar, 2 tablespoons sugar, and 1 tablespoon salt.

The 10 full cups of cooked rice should be sufficient to take care of four persons, even the hungriest of guests.

Preparation: Rice should be carefully washed, poured into a basket, and allowed to dry for three hours before cooking.

The water is first boiled and the rice added. Then reboiling takes place. When the rice is boiling hard, turn the flame down low to keep the water from bubbling over. Simmering for 10 minutes will give the rice the required consistency.

The rice, now cooked, should be placed in a large shallow bowl or platter and cooled by means of a fan. To half of the rice—the 5 cupfuls—is added the vinegar and salt amounts mentioned in A, and in a separate bowl to the remaining half is added the vinegar, sugar, and salt referred to in B.

A and B mixtures may be mingled together or kept apart, depending upon whether one wishes a sweet tart, or a sharp tart taste to the *sushi*.

There are three kinds of *sushi*, each distinctly different. They are called: *nigiri-zushi*, *norimaki-zushi*, and *chirashi-zushi*.

Nigiri-Zushi

This, the most common of the *sushi*, is a ball of sticky, boiled rice, treated with vinegar, topped with a bite of raw fish, perhaps first having been smeared with grated *wasabi*, or Japanese horseradish, a greenish strong-tasting substance to be used with care.

This rice-ball with its garnishings, truly a "rice-sandwich," is painted lightly with sugared *shoyu* and is eaten with chopsticks or fingers. Small slices of yellow ginger are served as a condiment.

The fish or shellfish to be used in *nigiri-zushi* are of

many kinds: sea-bream, tuna, prawn, shrimp, earshell, abalone, cuttlefish, flounder, sardine, etc.

Ingredients: 24 slices of the fish
24 balls of rice, approximately thumb-size in length, an inch in width, shaped ovally
5 teaspoons horseradish

Preparation: First the fish is sliced into rectangles a quarter-inch thick, an inch wide, and two inches long.

Take a scoop of rice in one hand and press it into a rough ovaloid. Spread its top length with a small amount of horseradish, evenly but not thickly. Top this with the strip of fish. Paint the top of the fish with *shoyu*, using a small bristly brush.

Sushi, generally served one pair at a time to an individual, are usually eaten with one or two slices of ginger, taken from a common receptacle where the thin slices rest in a tart liquid.

Japanese tea is almost always present, served in large cups. A Japanese likes to take a swallow from the cup to change the taste in his mouth between eating one type of *sushi* and another. This tea-serving practice may well be followed at home, especially if the housewife plans to serve several different kinds of *sushi*.

It is also recommended that the rice for the ball be prepared in a large Japanese rice-tub of a standard size readily purchasable in any Japanese hardware shop. It is easier to finger out the scoops of rice by this means.

A plain, watered-down piece of board—like a bread-cutting board—is recommended in making the rice into *sushi*.

It is better too that the hands be wet, or at least moist, since the rice and fish are sticky.

In similar fashion, one may prepare the whole range of *nigiri-zushi*, from prawns to scallops, from sea-bream to eels, keeping to the same dimensions of ingredients.

The horseradish, which is bought in a hard vegetable form, must be ground in the same way that one grinds cheese. It is mixed with just enough water to make it into a paste.

Nigiri-Zushi with Prawns

Special mention should be made of the recipe using shrimp or prawns in this *sushi* category, since, raw or cooked, they lend themselves wonderfully well to *nigiri-zushi*.

Ingredients: 12 prawns or shrimp (cut in half for 24 *sushi* pieces)
24 balls of rice
5 teaspoons horseradish

Preparation: Remove the shrimp heads and clean. Wash the flesh thoroughly with running water.

The shrimp or prawns may be used either raw or cooked. In either event, cut up into convenient sizes and proceed as described in the last recipe.

Nigiri-Zushi with Eels

This is another favorite among Japanese, and surprisingly many foreigners have taken to it with relish.

Ingredients: 2 long eels
24 balls of rice
5 teaspoons horseradish
A mixture of $1/2$ cup *shoyu*, $1/2$ cup *mirin*, and $1/2$ cup water

25

Preparation: Eels call for careful handling. They should be sliced but not cut all the way through; the belly of each is sliced open to permit removal of the bones. Eels are then boiled with *shoyu*, *mirin*, and water over a low flame.

Eels are then cut into convenient strips and combined with the rice. Finally, boil down the mixture in which the eels were originally cooked and pour it gently over the eel-rice combination.

Nigiri-Zushi with Eggs

Eggs, as well as fish and eels, can skilfully be combined with the seasoned rice to make a delectable rice-sandwich.

Ingredients: 2 eggs—both yolks and whites
1 1/2 ounces fish flesh
1 1/2 tablespoons sugar
1/2 teaspoon *shoyu*
1 pinch salt

Preparation: First, mash thoroughly the flesh of the fish to be used. Next, beat the eggs and mix with the *shoyu*, sugar, and salt.

Mix the flesh of the fish and the egg mixture, and fry together. Cut into rectangles.

Make *nigiri-zushi* in the usual fashion, putting one rectangle of egg, 1×2 inches, upon the boiled rice. Only in this case, one should omit the use of horse-radish.

Norimaki-Zushi

This too consists of sticky boiled and treated rice, with insertions, rolled up in Japanese edible seaweed or laver.

There are six different classes for this *norimaki-zushi*, in respect to ingredients.

Ingredients:

(1) 4 dried gourd shavings
$1/2$ teaspoon salt
2 tablespoons *shoyu*
$1 1/2$ tablespoons sugar
1 cup *dashi*

(2) $1/4$ cup soup brewed from dried gourd shavings
4 big mushrooms

$^1/_2$ tablespoon sugar

$^1/_2$ tablespoon *shoyu*

(3) $^1/_4$ pound spinach

$^1/_4$ teaspoon salt

$3^1/_2$ ounces white-flesh fish

2 eggs

$^1/_2$ teaspoon salt

1 tablespoon sugar

$1^1/_2$ tablespoons *sake*

(4) $1^1/_2$ ounces fish flesh or prawns

$1^1/_2$ tablespoons sugar

$^1/_4$ teaspoon salt

2 eggs

2 tablespoons *sake*

1 dash of coloring matter if desired

(5) 4 ounces red flesh fish

$^1/_4$ teaspoon salt

$^3/_4$ tablespoon sugar

$1^1/_2$ tablespoons *mirin*

(6) Usual amount of rice, cooked and steamed

3 cups water

$^1/_8$ cup vinegar

$^3/_4$ tablespoon sugar

$^1/_4$ teaspoon salt

Preparation: (1) Wash the dry gourd shavings in fresh water; then rewash in salted water. Boil these shavings until quite soft, using one full cup of *dashi* with sugar and salt added.

(2) First stem the dried mushrooms, then soften in warm water and slice into strips. Cook these in the mixture of the soup prepared from the dried gourd shavings, adding more *shoyu*, and more sugar to give the mixture its characteristic sweet-salty taste.

(3) Rinse the spinach and boil the leaves and the stems alike in salted water. Season eggs with sugar, salt, and *sake*, and fry. Then add spinach to fried mixture. Coat the fish with the light-fry mixture treated with the recommended flavorings, and cut the result into long strips, about $^1/_4$ inch wide.

(4) Fry the eggs and then add them, treated with salt, sugar, and *sake*, to the fish flesh. Beat in a mortar with a pestle.

(5) Boil the red-flesh fish and then crush with a pestle and mortar until the fish is a fine, granulated mass. Add sugar and salt.

The fish of both (4) and (5) is beaten in a mortar

29

until fluffy. Then the fish is lightly warmed in a fry pan over a low fire.

(6) Rice is cooked in the usual way and then rolled, with the foregoing ingredients inside it, onto an outer wrapping of seaweed as follows :

Lay one sheet of seaweed on a bamboo lattice, such as one can buy in any Japanese department store or see in any *sushi* shop, with the end of the seaweed strip even with the lattice end.

Spread the rice evenly and thickly on the seaweed sheet. On this rice, the gourd shavings, the prepared mushrooms, the boiled spinach and fish, the white-flesh fish, and the red-flesh fish are put, each layered on the other in long horizontal lines.

Then roll up the lattice like a coil, keeping the ingredients carefully in at both ends so that the seaweed encases all the inserted ingredients. Roll the lattice so that the seaweed is perfectly formed into a long cylinder by the pressure of the bamboo lattice, leaving a margin of seaweed to overlap.

Remove the lattice and cut the tightly-packed seaweed roll with a sharp knife, generally making eight cuts.

This *norimaki-zushi* is often served with the *nigiri-zushi*. It is also called *tekka-zushi*.

Chirashi-Zushi

This third general type of *sushi* employs the usual vinegared boiled rice, prepared with fish, vegetables, shrimp or prawns, dried fish, etc.

This is perhaps more complicated in regard to ingredients than the *norimaki-zushi*, needing no less than nine different classes of items.

Ingredients:

(1) 3½ cups rice, prepared with 3¾ cups water A sauce of ¼ cup vinegar, ¾ tablespoon salt, 2 tablespoons sugar

(2) 2 eggs, fried with 1½ teaspoons *dashi*, ⅛ teaspoon salt, and ¼ teaspoon sugar

(3) 1½ ounces kidney beans, seasoned with ¼ teaspoon salt and ¾ teaspoon sugar

(4) 1½ ounces canned tuna or salmon, prepared

with ³/₄ teaspoon *sake*,
¹/₈ teaspoon salt, and ³/₄
tablespoon sugar

(5) 3 ounces horse mackerel,
seasoned with ³/₄
tablespoon salt

(6) ¹/₂ ounce dried mush-
rooms

1¹/₂ ounces dried gourd
shavings

¹/₂ ounce beancurd, pre-
pared with ¹/₄ cup *dashi*,
3¹/₂ tablespoons *shoyu*,
3¹/₂ tablespoons sugar
as flavoring

(7) 2 ounces carrots, flavored
with 3 tablespoons
dashi, ¹/₄ teaspoon salt,
³/₄ tablespoon sugar

(8) 3 ounces lotus root or chestnuts, cooked with
³/₄ tablespoon vinegar,
³/₄ tablespoon sugar, ¹/₄
teaspoon salt

(9) Some slivered red ginger

Preparation: This also encompasses **nine** distinct steps.

(1) Boil rice with water. Strain and mix thoroughly with the sauce.

(2) Beat eggs thoroughly. Flavor with *dashi*, salt, and sugar. Fry the treated eggs lightly as an omelet.

(3) Boil the kidney beans in their skins, adding salt and sugar afterwards.

(4) Break up the canned fish into pieces from the original solid chunk. Place in a small bowl and set the bowl in a larger utensil of boiling water. Add the *sake*, salt, and sugar while this steaming is taking place.

(5) Salt the fish, rubbing the salt in well. Boil, and then mash when soft.

(6) Stem and soften the dried mushrooms in tepid water. Fragmentize them. Treat the dried gourd shavings in a similar fashion. Lightly wash the beancurd. Mix all three ingredients together and flavor with *dashi*, *shoyu*, and sugar.

(7) Wash, slice, and flavor the carrots.

(8) Peel the lotus roots or shell the chestnuts. Wash whichever is used carefully. Chop up the roots or the nuts, and then boil lightly with the vinegar, salt, and sugar.

(9) Wash and slice the ginger very thinly.

When these preparations have all been completed, four *domburi* are filled with the vinegared rice. On the rice place : the fried beancurd, mackerel, mushrooms, gourd shavings, and lotus roots or chestnuts ; then the beans, salmon bits, eggs ; and on top of all, the red, sliced ginger. The placement of the various ingredients in the foregoing manner is done purely for visual attactiveness.

If there is any difficulty in rolling the lattice for *norimaki-sushi*, in preparing *nigiri-zushi*, or in visualizing the final effect of the *chirashi-zushi*, by all means visit one of many thousands of *sushi* shops located throughout Japan and found in great abundance in any of the major cities. The proprietor will be glad to demonstrate.

The sign in Japanese ideographs for *sushi-ya* is not a hard one to recognize and can be copied down and committed to memory with profit.

Inside the shop is the bar of handsome, raw, unbarked, light wood at which the customers sit on stools. The shop owner awaits orders behind this bar. There is a big glass showcase displaying all the *sushi* ingredients. Also, in plain sight, is a large tub filled with vinegared rice. On the counter, next to water spigots, one finds bottles of soy sauce and bowls of

ginger with lattice lids. Tea is served immediately.
A small, squarish towel, hot in winter and cold in
summer, is served, twisted up, in a small bamboo tray.
This is a moist napkin for cleaning the hands and face.
These towels are known as *o-shibori* and foreigners take
to them readily.

It is the custom with those who are testing a new
sushi shop first to eat *nigiri-zushi* since it is believed—
even by *sushi* shop owners themselves—that this is a
very difficult type to make well. The point is that if
this can be made satisfactorily, all els ecan easily be
made to like satisfaction and with equal skill.

Sushi is indeed a Japanese favorite, being available
on Japanese railway platforms, in basket lunches, at
picnic grounds, almost everywhere. Foreigners too have
either liked *sushi* or else learned to like it.

Price is another recommendation. In the average
sushi-ya, a pair costs from 15 to 30 *yen*, rarely exceed-
ing 40 to 50 *yen* even in Tokyo's fancier places. *Norimaki-zushi*, served in sets of twelve pieces, costs about
100 to 200 *yen*.

Sushi doesn't take much time to prepare and it
does not cost a great deal. It always includes one main
item, discussion of which will be deferred until the
next chapter—raw fish.

4 RAW FISH

If *sushi* is the engagement, *sashimi*, or raw fish, is the wedding. Now is the time to stop dabbling and plunge boldly into what may be regarded as the *pièce de résistance*, in the accepted French sense, and what some may regard as just the piece to resist, others will regard as the one they cannot resist.

Raw fish, to many foreigners, spells trouble.

"Raw fish!" one can hear them scream, "how could anyone think of eating such a thing?"

Yet many do, foreigners as well as millions of Japanese. What after all are raw oysters, clams, and mussels but raw fish?

The trick is in getting used to thinking about actually eating raw fish. Mental preparation is what one needs, not a new stomach or a new set of nerves.

Sashimi is an acquired taste, but aren't beer, oysters, rice, whisky, spinach, frogs' legs, snails, sweetbreads, tripe, and liver?

There are two introductory schools: the Sink or Swim, and the Warned in Advance. Personally, I believe that unless I'd been tipped off ahead of time that someone was the unhappy owner of a queasy stomach I'd just serve the *sashimi* and its delicious sauce and say nothing until called upon to furnish more positive identification. In that way, social etiquette will dictate that guests at least sample everything served them, and thus will be avoided the first mental fright that might come if advance information is given out.

Once eaten, chances are strong that the guests will become devotees, despite themselves.

The Warned in Advance school, on the other hand, has to resort to contrivance—" Well, you've eaten raw oysters, haven't you?" or the even more defeatist—" Oh come on, just try it one time"—not realizing the poor psychological approach to those with natural prejudices who are perfectly capable of swallowing raw oysters without feeling the need to take on filets of raw fish.

So, take the fish by the gills, slice it, and serve it. It may be a dirty trick on the blissfully unsuspecting but you'll be forgiven. Eventual joy will come with the slow smile of delight spreading on the guest's face.

Regardless of viewpoint, *sashimi* is perhaps the

queen of Japanese delicacies, and no meal is complete without it. Get used to it if you can. Don't eat it if you don't want to. But you'll never wean any son of Japan, or daughter either, away from it.

So much for the introduction. Forward to the intimacies, with one additional word : *sashimi* can mean raw chicken as well as raw fish.

Sashimi itself is an artistic triumph, pleasing to the eye : the delicate red and gauzy-white tints of the fish flesh are in themselves appealing, but more so against the background of shredded white radish and a deep green patch of seaweed.

A long, narrow dish is usually used but it may be a round bowl. Japanese often capture nature and the artistic outdoors by using a plate resembling a fish in motion, a quiet river nook, or a deep pool. The fish itself, seen through the seaweed green, evokes the image of the creature swimming lazily through underwater reeds and roots. This is especially enchanting in summer when the whole effect of eating *sashimi*, complete with ice cubes, is both cooling and refreshing.

The beauty of the *sashimi* is that it lacks, oddly enough, both the fishy smell and fishy taste that would be its undoing. The taste is delicate, but enchanting, and there is no unpleasant smell.

Now, just what fish best lends itself to the *sashimi* treatment? Not all do. Japanese suggest these : seabream, tuna, cuttlefish, abalone—in general, any flatfish selected with a view to the season and geography. Shrimp and prawns also make wonderful *sashimi*. Best of all are the fish that come from the ocean, not the inland waters. Gourmets also like sardines.

Shoyu is the *sine qua non* of *sashimi*—eating *sashimi* without it would be like eating saltless bread.

Garnishing too is essential and comes in many varieties. Raw vegetables, grated or thinly sliced, may be used. Other ingredients are leaves of knot grass, parsley, lettuce, raw laver, or some small seed-spice.

For flavoring, since *sashimi* is odorless and very delicate, Japanese use horseradish, though a good foreign substitute would be hot mustard.

Now, the problem of the method of preparation faces the foreign housewife. And this is the best, simplest, and healthiest method :

First the fish is scaled, and head, tail, fins, and entrails are removed. The fish is washed carefully and allowed to soak in water. The flesh is divided laterally along the backbone, all bones are removed, and the upper and lower slices are halved again. All skin is removed. The flesh is now ready for slicing.

39

There are four ways of slicing the fish for *sashimi*:

(A) The usual way of cutting is to slice thin and place the slicings on a plate, overlapping each other, like roof tiles. Slicing is done at about a 30 degree angle with a very sharp, thin knife. The slices are cut to about the dimensions of potato slices prepared for the American home-fry treatment—$1\frac{1}{2}$ inches wide and $\frac{1}{2}$ inch thick.

(B) Fish with heavier meat lend themselves best to the dicing method of slicing—cubes of roughly $\frac{1}{2}$ to 1 inch in diameter.

(C) Conversely, fish with thin flesh is usually prepared in the thinnest of slicings, the knife held aslant, the flesh being whittled off evenly.

(D) Long fish must be regarded differently, the length of the entire fish first being cut into three portions. Then these sections are cut like a loaf of bread, slantwise into pieces $\frac{1}{4}$ to $\frac{1}{2}$ inch in width.

Raw Fish Filets

And now we come to the actual preparation of a standard fish for *sashimi*.

Ingredients: 1 pound sea-bream, tuna, or other flatfish

> Small handful of parsley,
> watercress, etc.
> 1½ teaspoons horseradish
> or grated ginger
> 4 tablespoons *shoyu.*

Preparation: First, the fish is sliced, as has been described, with all slices being transferred to the platter, next to the green leaves. The horse-radish (or ginger) is mixed with the *shoyu*, and the fish slices are dipped into the mixture and eaten.

Other fish are prepared and eaten the same way.

Boiled *Sashimi*

This is somewhat rare. Hot water is first poured over the raw fish, and the fish is then eaten with vinegar. The fish surface has not been cooked, but only scalded. The taste, however, is slightly different. Hygiene may be somewhat more assured but, the author hastens to say, raw fish itself is *not* unsanitary. As in the case of any food, care should be exercised to select fresh fish from sanitary fishmongers and in the proper season.

Lobster, Shrimp, or Prawn Filets

The second major *sashimi* classification deals with lobster, shrimp, or prawns.

> **Ingredients:** 2 medium-size live prawns
> or 4 live shrimp
> Some greens
> Some seaweed or thinly sliced cabbage or carrots
> 1½ teaspoons horseradish or 3½ teaspoons grated ginger
> 4 tablespoons *shoyu*.

Preparation: This is done somewhat differently from the fish filets. First, a knife is plunged into the soft belly while the creature lives, thus killing quickly and painlessly. The shell is removed and the inside quivering flesh thoroughly washed. When this flesh stiffens in the cold, running water, stop washing and dry off.

Boil the shell and when it becomes its characteristic red color, in cold water, put the meat back into its boiled shell for serving.

Put the grated horseradish, or grated ginger,

seaweed, and garnishing greens around the shellfish—
greens against the red for color and atmosphere—and
serve with a small side plate of *shoyu* mixed with horseradish. The prawn or shrimp chunks are dipped in
to this mixture and eaten.

Boiled Shrimp or Prawn *Sashimi*

This is still another dish featuring prawns or
shrimp.

Ingredients: 8 ounces shrimp or prawns
8 ounces cucumbers
2 ounces thinly-sliced cabbage
1½ teaspoons horseradish
or 3½ tablespoons pow-
dered ginger
¼ cup *shoyu*

Preparation: The cabbage, is dipped
quickly into scalding water, and allowed to dry.

Wash and peel the cucumbers, cut uniformly into
¼ inch cubes.

The shrimp or prawns are then boiled in salt water
for about 5 minutes.

Fish, cucumber, and cabbage are served together in small bowls, with side dishes of *shoyu* (mixed with horseradish or ginger). The prawns or shrimp are first dipped into this mixture and then eaten.

Chicken *Sashimi*

One doesn't have to associate with raw fish entirely. One can also turn with relish to raw chicken.

Ingredients: 6 ounces white chicken meat

8 ounces cucumbers

2 ounces sliced cabbage or carrots

1½ teaspoons horseradish or 3½ teaspoons of grated ginger

¼ cup *shoyu*

Preparation: After slicing the chicken meat thin, the slices are dipped into boiling water, as in the foregoing recipe, then quickly dipped in cold water.

Cucumber, cabbage, or carrot slices are prepared as in the foregoing recipe and served with the chicken slices. The chicken slices are dipped into the usual mixture of *shoyu* and horse radish, or ginger, and then eaten.

Fugu Sashimi

The housewife should be strictly advised against preparing this dish by herself, since *fugu*, wrongly prepared, can be deadly, however tasty. This blowfish is best prepared at licensed places by licensed chefs.

Still, with the poison drained off, there is no question but that this puffer is a delicacy.

It should be tried at least once, and in the *sashimi* style of serving. The sauce is especially notable—a thinner *shoyu* is used, with small cut-up pieces of Japanese leek inserted for flavor, and with just a slight dash of vinegar or lemon juice.

5
THIRST-QUENCHERS

If rice is the staple food of the Japanese stomach, then surely tea serves the same purpose for the Japanese throat. No book on Japanese cooking would be complete without reference to this tea.

Furthermore, Japanese cooking, replete with spices and sauces, however mild, is thirst-provoking, so that tea and other liquids are consumed in relatively large quantities.

Next to tea in importance comes *sake*, the Japanese rice wine, usually served hot and never absent from any feast. Water is taken rarely, tea being preferred. Coffee, however, has its many devotees.

Tea in Japan is green. It is served ceremonially as powdered tea called *matcha*. And all Japanese tea is served without sugar, cream, milk, or lemon.

The best tea is called *gyokuro* (literally "gem-dew"), followed by *aoyagi* or *aoyanagi*, and by still coarser types such as *sen-cha* and *ban-cha*. There is a special tea called *habu-cha*, a seaweed tea known as *kombu-cha*, and the black, imported foreign tea called *ko-cha*. A pleasant summer drink is *mugi-cha*, which is brewed from roasted wheat kernels boiled in water. It is served cold, with or without sugar.

Green tea is not so simple to prepare as most believe. Its taste depends on the quality of tea leaves used, the kind and amount of charcoal used for heating the tea water, the nature and temperature of this water, and even on the sort sort of utensils used.

To brew ordinary tea properly, one should follow the local custom. A Japanese teapot may be just large enough for two or three small cups of tea, or it may be large enough for five or six. In any case, the pot is emptied at each serving to keep the tea from becoming bitter. A scant teaspoon of tea is used for each cup. If the tea is very delicate, the water should be just under boiling; if less delicate, the water may be bubbling quickly. The tea is put in the pot, the water added, allowed to rest a moment, swirled gently to dampen all the leaves well, and then poured. Additional water is not added until more tea is wanted. This preserves the fragrance of the liquid, and prevents the tea from becoming bitter.

Japanese make a fine grade of beer, including stout

or black beer, but the native alcoholic beverages are: *sake*, made from the best rice; and *shochu*, distilled from inferior rice or sweet potatoes.

There are two special kinds of *sake* : *mirin*, used in cooking, and *toso*, which is served on ceremonial and special holiday occasions.

Just a word on this last. The brewing methods used in making *toso* are a closely guarded secret. All that is known is that certain spices and a small amount of a medical herb-powder are used. The distillers will also say this one thing more: that the powders are placed in a triangular silk bag sold at drugstores. The bag is then soaked in the *toso*. This special brand may be found in any liquor store, primarily during the winter months.

Toso has been prepared since the Heian period of Japanese history. It is served to prolong life, insure happiness, and to avoid evil and harm.

And now let us turn to a different category of liquids—the soups of Japan, some thirst-quenching, others thirst-provoking, all new taste experiences.

6
SOUPS

There are two kinds of Japanese soups: *suimono*, or clear soup; and *misoshiru*, or thick, heavy soup. The first uses meat or fish with vegetables, and is flavored with salt, *shoyu*, and *dashi*; the second consists of fish, meat, vegetables, and bean curd and is flavored with *miso*, the fermented bean paste.

In both types of soup Japanese often use some *sake* or dry cooking sherry for flavoring. Sometimes, as extra flavoring, they also use Japanese pepper-plant buds, ginger, or lemon juice.

The standard vegetables employed are marsh parsley, leeks, watercress, chinese or snow peas, spinach, and the fragrant herb known as *shungiku*.

There is also a special New Year's soup called *zoni*, which will be described later. Also several fine fish or chicken chowders are included in Japanese soups.

Clam Soup

Let's start with the clear soup recipes. Here is a simple, delicious clam soup. But clams are naturally salty, so take care!

Ingredients: 8 large or 16 small clams
3 1/2 cups water
1 tablespoon *shoyu*
1 teaspoon salt
3/4 teaspoon *sake*

Preparations: Clams should first be thoroughly washed and rinsed; then put in a saucepan of boiling water and boil until the shells crack. Season with the salt, *sake*, and *shoyu*. Serve as a garnish a leaf of Japanese pepper or a slice of lemon rind.

Chicken Soup

This is a splendid combination of chicken, thin noodles, and mushrooms which will satisfy the most discerning taste.

Ingredients: 4 ounces chicken
1 1/2 ounces *udon* (Japanese noodles)
12 large mushrooms
3 1/2 cups *dashi*

1 1/2 teaspoons salt
1 1/2 teaspoons *shoyu*
4 pieces lemon peel

Preparation: The chicken should first be sliced, put in hot water, and allowed to boil. When it is tender the precooked noodles are added, then the *dashi*, salt, and *shoyu*. Lastly, the mushrooms are added, these having been previously cooked. Pieces of chicken and mushrooms are placed in the individual serving bowls, and the soup stock is poured over them. Lastly, a piece of lemon rind is used as a garnish in each bowl of soup.

Egg Soup

The housewife will enjoy preparing this unique departure from the Western way of treating eggs. This dish is similar to what the Chinese know as chicken-and-egg-drop soup.

Ingredients: 2 eggs
1 piece ginger
1 piece parsley
Soup base from 5 cups *dashi*
2 teaspoons cornstarch

2 teaspoons salt

2 teaspoons *shoyu*

Preparation: The soup stock is first boiled, with the liquid mixture of cornstarch, *shoyu*, and salt, then simmered. Eggs are beaten frothy and spread with a perforated dipper over the simmering soup surface, so that they float, not sink. Sliced or grated ginger is added, then parsley.

Bean Curd Soup

Eastern and Western vegetables here combine to furnish a delicate but balanced soup.

Ingredients: 6 ounces of *tofu* or bean curd

1 leek

Handful spinach

1½ teaspoons sliced ginger

4 cups *dashi*

1¾ teaspoons salt

¾ tablespoon *shoyu*

Preparation: Dice the *tofu* and cut the spinach and leeks up fine. Boil the *dashi* with the salt, *shoyu*, bean curd, and vegetables. Add ginger before serving.

A similar type of soup may be made with eggs instead of bean curd, as follows :

Ingredients: 2 eggs
³/₄ teaspoon salt
¹/₄ teaspoon *shoyu*
Soup base from 5 cups *dashi*
2 ounces spinach or Japanese *shungiku*

Preparation: This soup uses beaten eggs. Add the *dashi*, salt, and *shoyu* to the eggs and allow the whole mixture to simmer over a low flame. The greens are added, these having been precooked separately a few minutes before serving.

Codfish & Vegetable Soup

Fish, spinach, and dried mushrooms prepared together make a tasty soup for fish-lovers.

Ingredients: 6 ounces codfish, or other white-flesh fish
³/₄ teaspoon salt
2¹/₂ ounces spinach
4 ounces dried mushrooms

2 1/2 tablespoons *dashi*
1/4 teaspoon *shoyu*
1/2 teaspoon more salt
1/2 teaspoon more *shoyu*
2 1/2 cups more *dashi*
4 pieces lemon peel

Preparation: Salt the fish well, then cut into four equal pieces and boil. Slice the spinach into inch lengths and boil separately. Soften the stemmed mushrooms and lightly boil; then add the *dashi*, *shoyu*, and salt. Now place a piece of fish, some spinach, and some mushroom pieces together in each bowl and pour the hot flavored water, in which the mushrooms have been boiled, over these. Heat the extra amounts of *dashi* and *shoyu* and fill the bowls of each guest. Add a piece of lemon rind to each bowl before serving.

Fish Stew

This is a delicious and filling stew, the equal of anything to be found along the Maine or California coasts.

Ingredients: 1 pound cod, sea-bream, tuna, or halibut
3/4 pound bean curd
4 dried mushrooms

1 leek
Soup stock from 3 1/2 cups
   dashi
1/4 teaspoon sweet vinegar
   or lemon juice
1/2 teaspoon *shoyu*

Preparation: Dice the bean curd. Then slice the mushrooms lengthwise. Remove all fish bones and slice the fish into big, thick slices. Boil the *dashi* with bones, head, entrails, and fins.

Add the mushrooms, the bean curd, and the fish to the boiled soup stock and allow to cook. Serve the stew in small serving bowls with a side sauce of cut-up leek soaked in the vinegar, or lemon, and *shoyu* mixture. Dip into this mixture the larger chunks of fish or vegetables before eating.

Chicken or Fish Chowder

Japan boasts of its chowders, no less than does the American from Maine or the Frenchman from Marseilles.

Ingredients: 3/4 pound either chicken or
   fish
   1/4 teaspoon salt

1/4 pound fish paste, or
kamaboko

1/4 pound broiled sea-eel

3/4 pound leafy vegetables
(spinach, lettuce, cab-
bage)

3 small bundles Japanese
noodles

1/4 pound either potatoes
or chestnuts

8 dried mushrooms

20 gingko nuts or Brussels
sprouts

4 cups *dashi* mixed with 1/2
cup *shoyu*

Preparation: First slice the chicken or
fish and sprinkle with salt. Slice the boiled fish paste
and cut the eel into suitable cooking lengths. Cut the
tubers, the leafy vegetables, and the noodles into convenient sizes.

Soften the dried mushrooms in tepid water after
stemming. Lightly boil the nuts or the sprouts and
set to one side. Now, pour two cups of *dashi* into a
saucepan, adding 1/4 cup *shoyu*, and boil the potatoes

in this mixture. After boiling, add the chicken or fish, the mushrooms, the spinach, the eel, the gingko nuts, the fish paste, and the Japanese noodles. Place the lid on the sauce pan and reboil.

Preparations for a second round may be achieved by adding the rest of the *dashi*.

Oyster Soup

Oyster soup has its devotees all over the world, no less in Japan where the preparation is somewhat more exotic.

Ingredients: 8 ounces oysters
3 cups *dashi*
$3/4$ teaspoon cornstarch
$1/2$ teaspoon either red pepper or tabasco

Preparation: Take the oysters from their shells and wash the meat in cold running water. Boil the *dashi* and gradually add the oysters. When this is thoroughly cooked add the cornstarch mixed with a little cold water. The pepper is used for flavoring.

Boiled Chicken Stew

This is what Japanese universally know and relish as *tori no mizutaki*.

Ingredients: 1 tender chicken

12 cups water

1 leek

Sauce composed of ½ cup of juice from bitter orange or ½ cup lemon juice, ¾ cup *shoyu*, and 1½ tablespoons salt

Preparation: First carefully pluck the chicken, and remove all entrails. Cut the meat from the bones. Boil the chicken in 12 cups of water over a low fire. Simmer the mixture until done. Remove the bones when done. Add the *shoyu* to the bitter orange or lemon juice.

Cut the leek lengthwise, slice or chop it, and add to the chicken. Mix the *shoyu*-lemon sauce and the salt with the simmering chicken-leek mixture and allow to cook until the chicken chunks are very soft. For an individual touch serve in separate soup bowls. Keep

extra salt in small side dishes and parch to keep it fine.
Dip the pieces of chicken in the extra salt, if desired.

Pork & Vegetable Soup

Pork is second only to beef and chicken as a favorite Japanese soup ingredient, and in this soup, served with vegetables, it is especially delicious.

Ingredients: 6 ounces fat pork
8 dried mushrooms
4 ounces spinach or leeks
1 fat carrot
1 bamboo shoot
Soup base from 4 cups *dashi*, 1 teaspoon salt, 1 teaspoon *shoyu*, and a small amount of grated ginger

Preparation: Pork, mushrooms, carrots, and bamboo shoots are all sliced very thin. The soup base is warmed, flavored with salt and *shoyu*, and the vegetables are added. The entire mixture is boiled, and then the pork strips are added. Lastly, the spinach or leeks are added and boiled. The piping-hot soup

is served in individual bowls. More ginger may be
added as extra flavoring.

Vegetable & Shrimp Soup

Shrimp or prawns combine with turnips or radishes
to make a tantalizingly different dish.

Ingredients: 6 ounces shrimp
$\frac{1}{2}$ teaspoon salt
$\frac{1}{2}$ teaspoon sugar
1 beaten egg
$\frac{1}{2}$ pound either turnips or
radishes
$\frac{1}{2}$ teaspoon salt for vegetables
2 tablespoons *sake* or dry
cooking sherry
8 dried mushrooms
Handful spinach
Soup base from $4\frac{1}{2}$ cups
dashi, 1 teaspoon salt,
and 1 teaspoon *shoyu*

Preparation: The shrimp are shelled
and minced. Sugar and salt, followed by the egg, are

mixed with the shrimp. The turnips or radishes are sliced or diced, then mixed with the *sake* and salt and added to the shrimp and egg mixture.

Mushrooms are stemmed and, with the spinach, are softened in tepid water. After these vegetables have become soft, they are cooked in the soup base. The shrimp and egg mixture is added to the soup base and the entire mixture is allowed to simmer until done.

Put pieces of shrimp, two mushrooms, and some of the spinach into a soup bowl and pour the soup mixture over these. Serve hot.

Vegetable & Egg Soup

This is a light soup, nutritious and tasty, which can be made with little effort.

Ingredients: 4 eggs
3 ½ cups *dashi*
1 cucumber or
5 ounces green peas or fresh beans
1 ½ teaspoons *shoyu*
1 ½ teaspoons salt

Preparation: Heat the *dashi* and season with salt and *shoyu*. Peel and slice the cucumber, or shell and wash the peas or beans. Boil the vegetable in the *dashi* soup base. Break the eggs over the boiling vegetable. *Do not stir*. The soup, a composition of eggs and vegetables cooked in *dashi* soup stock, is served individually.

Lobster *Bisque*

Lobster is one of Japan's great delicacies. Any soup using it is assured of success.

Ingredients: 1 whole lobster or two large prawns
1 teaspoon salt
5 cups *dashi*
Handful of small leeks and marsh parsley, cabbage, and lettuce (leeks and cabbage alone will suffice)
2 teaspoons salt
2 teaspoons *shoyu*

Preparation: Cut off the lobster's head and cut the body into four sizable chunks. Boil 2 cups of water and add the teaspoon of salt. Then place the lobster, piece after piece, and the greens, sliced to make cooking easier, into the boiling, salted water. Boiled, the lobster and greens alike are salted, seasoned with *shoyu*, and placed in bowls. The heated *dashi* stock is poured over all.

Boiled Lobster Soup

Quite differently prepared but none the less delicious is this lobster variation in the form of soup.

Ingredients: 6 ounces lobster
$^3/_4$ teaspoon salt
2 small cucumbers
8 dried mushrooms
$^1/_4$ cup *dashi*
$^3/_4$ teaspoon *shoyu*
A soup base of $3^3/_4$ cups *dashi*, $^3/_4$ teaspoon salt, and $^3/_4$ teaspoon *shoyu*
4 pieces lemon rind

Preparation: Take the lobster from its shell, salt, mince, and boil. Add gradually $^3/_4$ teaspoon *shoyu* and $^1/_4$ cup *dashi* to the boiling lobster.

Peel the two cucumbers and slice thin. Then stem the mushrooms and soften in lukewarm water. Boil separately with ¼ cup of *dashi* and ¾ teaspoon of salt. Pieces of cucumber, boiled lobster, and mushrooms are placed in soup bowls. Then the main soup mixture of the *dashi*, the salt, and the *shoyu* is heated and poured over these. Lemon rind is floated on top of each bowl.

This completes the clear soup range. Now let us turn to that of the *misoshiru*, the thick heavy soup that is prepared from fermented bean paste which is colored either red or white.

But first, what exactly is *miso*, or bean paste?

Its origin is crushed soybeans, boiled and preserved in a kind of yeast and allowed to stand until fermented. Good *miso* is kept on hand for many years, since the longer it is preserved, the more matured it becomes.

There are several standard types of *misoshiru*—oyster, fish, vegetable, potato, and shellfish.

Oyster *Miso*

We have perhaps sampled the oyster soup made

from *dashi*. Now to try the broth prepared with *miso*.

Ingredients: 8 ounces oysters
3 ½ ounces *miso*
3 cups *dashi*
¾ teaspoon cornstarch
½ teaspoon powdered red
or grey pepper or ¼
teaspoon Tabasco sauce

Preparation: Remove the oysters from their shells and wash carefully. Boil the combination of *miso* and *dashi*, and gradually add the oysters to the mixture. Mix the cornstarch with water and add this to the treated oysters, now swimming in the *miso-dashi* liquid. Simmer until done. Flavor with red pepper or Tabasco sauce just before serving.

Fish & Vegetable *Miso*

This soup combines white-flesh sea-bream, or *tai*, the greatest Japanese fish delicacy, with succulent vegetables.

Ingredients: 6 ounces sea-bream or
other white-flesh fish

6 ounces bean curd
1 leek
4 ounces *miso*
4 cups *dashi*

Preparation: First boil the white-flesh fish and the bean curd. Boil the *miso* and *dashi* and add the fish and the bean curd. Mince the leek and feed into the boiling mixture. Simmer until done. Serve individually.

Potato Miso

The old American-style potato soup was never like this. Once eaten, never forgotten.

Ingredients: 6 ounces pork or chicken
1 ½ ounces carrots
1 ½ ounces leeks
2 ½ ounces sweet potatoes
½ ounce burdock
Soup base of 4 ounces *miso* and 4 cups *dashi*

Preparation: First boil the *miso* and *dashi*, then add the pork or chicken strips, followed by sliced or diced carrots, burdock, and potatoes. Last, add the leeks and simmer the soup until done.

Shrimp or Prawn *Miso*

Here is a shrimp or prawn soup, made with *miso* and considered pleasing both visually and taste-wise.

Ingredients: 6 ounces shrimp or prawns
6 ounces bean curd
4 ounces *miso*
3 cups *dashi*
Some ginger

Preparation: Shell the seafood and mince with one teaspoon of *miso*. Boil the rest of the *miso* with *dashi* and add the shellfish and the bean curd. Cook these together and when done, strain. Place the cooked fish and bean curd into individual bowls and pour the cooked *miso-dashi* mixture over these. Add ginger to taste and serve individually.

Japanese *Zoni*

This is a Japanese specialty, known for being served at New Year's when it is the acknowledged holiday soup. It takes some skill and a rather large number of ingredients to prepare, none of them difficult to obtain, however.

Ingredients: 3 1/2 ounces white chicken meat

$^3/_4$ teaspoon cornstarch

1 large piece *kamaboko*,
or fish paste

1 carrot

3 pieces taro root

$^1/_2$ cup *dashi*

$^1/_4$ teaspoon *shoyu*

$^1/_4$ teaspoon salt

1 $^1/_2$ to 2 ounces garden
spinach

4 pieces lemon rind

8 pieces glutinous rice-
cake

Mixture of 4 cups *dashi*,
$^3/_4$ tablespoon salt, and
$^3/_4$ tablespoon *shoyu*

Some Japanese herbs
called *nanakusa*

Preparation: Japanese tradition calls for *wakamizu*, or young water, drawn from the well just as the new year dawns. This may be omitted.

Slice the chicken into slivers, eight pieces to serve four persons. Sprinkle the chicken meat with corn-starch and flatten the treated flesh with a cleaver to make larger. Boil the chicken in very hot water.

Slice the fish paste into eight pieces, each a quarter-inch thick.

Cut the carrot into cherry-flower-petal shapes and prepare eight pieces for decoration.

Peel the taro roots and slice them from end to end into pieces about one quarter-inch thick. Make 12 slices in all.

Boil the carrot and the root with the *dashi*. When soft, flavor with *shoyu* and salt.

Boil the spinach. Take out while still green and cut into inch lengths.

Slice the lemon rind into thin slivers.

The rice cakes, which the Japanese call *o-mochi*, are essential to New Year's. These glutinous balls of rice have been made by pounding rice for several days. They are toasted gently around the edges. The housewife may save herself time and effort by buying these at a market.

Boil the *dashi*, *shoyu*, and salt.

Put two rice cakes into each guest's bowl, adding the chicken slivers, the fish paste, the vegetables, taro, herbs if used, and some lengths of boiled spinach. Pour over everything the hot flavored mixture of *dashi*, salt, and *shoyu*. Serve the soup with a piece of lemon rind floating on top.

7

ROASTED ON A PLOUGH

Foreigners, thinking primarily of the Japanese soups, are prone to criticize Japanese food as being too light, too flimsy, dainty and unfilling.

This criticism will soon disappear if the guest is served *sukiyaki*, the favorite Japanese dish with most foreigners, and an increasing favorite of the Japanese themselves, as they become more accustomed to eating meat.

But what exactly is *sukiyaki*?

The word derives from two Japanese ideographs—the first, *suki*, meaning plough, the second, *yaki*, meaning roasted or plough-roasted—roasted on a plough.

Even in Great Britain and the United States, there is a notion that the most delectable bacon, ham, etc., is that which has been fried on a flat surface, or as laborers insist, on the flat surface of a spade. Laborers will argue that no cleaner cooking surface exists than the blade of a tool recently plunged into fresh earth.

Japanese farmers have likewise long maintained that this is so, frying from time immemorial their meats not on spades, which were rarely used in olden times, but on the blades of their ploughs.

Buddhist conceptions enter the picture also, for old-time farmers believed that not only flesh-eating was forbidden as a Buddhist sin, but also that the sauce was to be abjured since it was too succulent and thus became a temptation to be avoided. Human nature, so often in defiance of tradition and decree, eventually yielded.

All this, fortunately, has been changed so much that Japanese, no less than foreigners, can dine with relish on this once-forbidden food.

Bear in mind that every bit of cooking is done before the diner's eyes. Guests may thus be freed from fears of the unseen dangers that might lurk in an unseen, unsanitary kitchen. The diner may also smell the captivating odors that arise from this dish as it cooks.

Sukiyaki may be served on a Western table, but somehow it is not the proper setting for this Oriental concoction. If at all possible, the housewife should attempt to create some of the authentic Japanese atmosphere.

The guests should sit on cushions on the straw-matted floor, cross-legged around a low, round table.

In the middle of this round table is either an electric heater, a small gas stove, or, in the pure Japanese style, a traditional charcoal cooking brazier. The pan or cooking utensil rests on top of the brazier.

The various ingredients are placed on platters in the immediate vicinity of the cooking apparatus. Meat, beef usually, is of supreme importance and it must be fresh, tender, and sliced very thin with just a little fat clinging to each meat shred. The best *sukiyaki* beef is both lean and fat.

Next in importance are the vegetables: the long green leeks, the white bean curd squares, the fat onions, the burdock, the small bundles of Japanese vermicelli, the tree mushrooms if in season, the bamboo sprouts, bean shoots, and whatever else may be desired. One can use foreign-style vegetables, such as spinach, carrots, or radishes, or rely on Japanese vegetables, such as *seri*, or parsley; *mitsuba*, or marsh parsley; *konnyaku* or devilsfoot squares; or *gobo*, or edible burdock.

Three important liquids are used in preparing *sukiyaki*: water, *shoyu*, and fine grade *sake*. Water is usually mixed with the sugar, although it is just as proper to sprinkle sugar on the meat and vegetables while they are simmering in the *nabe*, or frying pan.

Since the dish needs many ingredients and since mixing in correct proportions is a requisite to proper taste, it might be wise at this point to list the ingredients to be used.

The following utensils are needed should one wish to serve *sukiyaki* at home:

- 1 round table, wide enough so that two persons would be able to shake hands across it without strain
- 1 heater or *hibachi*, the Japanese earthenware cooking pot. (Or gas stove or large-coil electric stove)
- 1 shallow, thick, metal saucepan, large enough for all ingredients
- 1 big platter for meat and the green leeks
- 1 pitcher for *shoyu*
- 1 jug for *sake*
- 2 or 3 big spoons for stirring
- 1 pair of large chopsticks
- 4 individual bowls
- 4 individual chopsticks and 4 chopstick-rests
- 4 saucers
- 4 napkins or bibs

The liquid ingredients in the following list are in amounts required for the first saucepan of *sukiyaki*.

More shoyu, sake, dashi, and water are used for subsequent servings.

Ingredients: 16 ounces sukiyaki beef (32 ounces for heavily eating guests)

12 tablespoons shoyu

8 tablespoons sugar

1 cup dashi

4 teaspoons sake

1 big bunch of leeks (10 or 12 in a bunch)

6 average-size round onions

16 to 20 average-size mushrooms

16 ounces bean curd

2 long pieces of burdock root

6 bundles of shirataki, or Japanese vermicelli

1 raw egg per guest

Preparation: First the housewife must heat the main pan, greasing the surface with a large piece of fat until it sizzles and the pan becomes coated with fat.

The first ingredient to be used is some *shoyu*; next add some sugar to redress the tart balance. *Sukiyaki* itself is a happy mixture of sweet and tart. After the sugar comes a dash, maybe two, of *sake.*

Many cooks argue that vegetables should precede the meat into the pan, and equally as many insist on the reverse. Meat juices acting on vegetables, vegetable juices on meat, it makes little difference. The majority opinion seems to favor the entrance of vegetables before the meat and in this order: leeks, onion slices, burdock slivers, the Japanese vermicelli, the bean curd, and then the other vegetables.

While these are browning and exuding their delicious aroma, the cook places the strips of meat on the vegetable-sauce cushion to cook. Allow this to simmer for about 15 minutes.

The guests, attentively watching, may now get ready. They may split apart their individual chopsticks and may break open and froth up the individual raw eggs placed in a bowl at each place.

A word about these eggs enjoyed by most diners, foreign as well as Japanese. Two things should be born in mind, especially in the squeamish mind. First, the egg has a bland flavor, and next, it is half cooked almost at once by the entry of the well-cooked meat and vegetables into the same saucer.

The egg has many uses. Among others it serves to cool the piping hot meat and vegetables.

Try it once and if you don't like it, then never again. Once tasted though, it is usually never forsaken.

The meat strips should be closely watched, for as soon as one side is browned they should be reversed in the pan, allowing the other side to brown equally.

Guests should be served as soon as the meat is done, for leaving the meat and vegetables in the hot, bubbling juices too long will dissipate part of the delicately balanced flavor. More meat and vegetables are added to the sauce after the first serving, and these simmer while the guests enjoy their first helpings.

Sugar or sugared water, *shoyu*, and *sake* are added from time to time to correct the balance and to ensure a proper mixture of sweet and tart.

Now, how is *sukiyaki* served?

The dish is not so much a single food item as it is the main part of an extensive Japanese dinner. One rarely if ever eats *sukiyaki* alone, either from the standpoint of other dishes or of other people.

The repast begins with a clear soup and is accompanied by either warmed *sake* or cold beer, these to be served throughout the meal, since the sugar and *shoyu* used in the *sukiyaki* are guaranteed to raise a thirst.

The other dishes that are served are rice and dessert; the latter usually consists of seasonal fruits. The hostess should always remember to serve white rice with or after *sukiyaki*. Foreigners generally like their rice served simultaneously so that they can spoon the delicious sauce-gravy over it, though to the Japanese this is unthinkable.

A word about the cost of ingredients may be of interest to the housewife. All prices are reasonably steady on the Japanese market.

Meat, the main item, will run from 400 to 600 *yen* for four persons, depending on the cuts chosen. Eggs are priced between 10 and 20 yen each, depending on size and season. Vegetables usually range from 10 to 50 *yen* for each vegetable of the proper amount for four servings. *Shoyu, dashi*, sugar, and *sake* are generally on hand in the average household, even many foreign ones.

A fine *sukiyaki* dinner, complete with soup, rice, and fruits, with both *sake* and beer, should not cost more than two thousand *yen*, or between $5 and $6.50 per four individuals.

It should also be remembered that while *sukiyaki* immediately suggests beef, it is not necessarily confined to beef. Chicken, duck, pork, game, or even oysters may be used.

However, Japanese call some of these combinations by different names: the chicken mixture is colled *tori-nabe* and the oyster dish is *hamanabe*.

Other variants of *sukiyaki*, while still in the meat and vegetable classification, have local names and significances. One that quickly leaps to mind is what Nagoya citizens term *batayaki*. This is a meat or chicken *suki-yaki* treated in the "ploughcooked" way, but using a large amount of butter in the cooking instead of only a sugar-*shoyu-sake* sauce.

One may also find, in Osaka and Tokyo particularly, a game-type *sukiyaki*-style cooking known as *kabutoyaki*, or cooked on a helmet; also *okaribayaki*, or in an open skillet, hunting style.

These variations use the same ingredients as other *sukiyaki* recipes but the meat and vegetables are individually grilled instead of being boiled together in a sauce.

Helmet-Roasted

Ingredients: 16 ounces sliced beef (32
for heavy eaters)
1 big bunch of leeks
16 to 20 mushrooms
2 large stalks burdock
½ pound spinach leaves
8 fat onions
8 to 12 pieces of *konnyaku*,
a tuberous root paste
8 to 12 fat slices of white
potato
1 cup *dashi*
A sauce for four indi-
vidual bowls composed
of 1 cup *shoyu*, ½ cup
sake, ⅛ cup vinegar, 2
tablespoons sugar, 1
teaspoon salt, and 4
pinches grey or red
pepper.
4 saucers grated radish

Preparation: Use a convex-shaped grill,
perforated with many holes and fired by gas or a large

79

charcoal pot underneath. First wipe the grill surface thoroughly with fat. Then, as it sizzles, lay the strips of meat painted quickly with *dashi* on the grill face for cooking. Meat strips will be followed by vegetables cut into suitable lengths: the leeks, mushrooms, onion slices, potato slices, spinach leaves and *konnyaku* squares. Each may be painted quickly with *dashi* taken from a nearby receptacle.

The sauce into which the meat and vegetables are dipped before eating is served in accompanying saucers. The ingredients mentioned above will generally suffice for the needs of four average people. One should mix the *shoyu*, vinegar, sugar, salt, and *sake* to one's individual taste, and shredded radishes, a drop or two of lemon juice, a sprinkling of red or gray pepper, or the Japanese *wasabi*, green-colored horseradish, may be mixed with this sauce. These ingredients, at any event, should be on hand to permit the guest to select what he wishes.

When the sauce is ready, the guest may take the roasted strips of meat and vegetables from the grill surface. These are dipped into the prepared sauce and eaten.

Any hot iron slab, fired by gas or charcoal, will suffice, although the best results are obtained by using a convex grill of stainless steel, perforated with many round holes through which cooking gases may seep.

The other dishes in the roasted food range will be taken up in the next chapter.

8
SKEWERS
&
GRILLS

Skewering and grilling fish, meat, shellfish, eels, and various vegetables are the featured Japanese ways of preparing roasted foods.

In ordinary cases the food to be cooked will first be sprinkled with salt, or dipped first in a *dashi-shoyu* mixture. The cooked food is often eaten after a pepper sprinkling, or even after being dipped in a light *shoyu* sauce, seasoned by sweet vinegar or lemon juice. Foods which are treated with *shoyu* are prepared in the following manner : mix 1/4 cup *shoyu*, 1/4 cup *sake*, and 1/4 cup *dashi* in a large bowl and paint the vegetables and meats with this sauce before skewering or grilling.

There are some who prefer broiling the food after it has been soaked in *miso* sauce. Foods which are treated with *miso*, the bean paste liquid, are soaked for two or three days in the *miso* before skewering or roasting.

This second method is used mostly for fish, eels,

shrimp, prawns, chicken, game birds and the like.

The first, and perhaps most celebrated dish to be discussed, is roasted chicken, or what the Japanese call *yakitori*.

Spitted Chicken

This is especially favored by foreigners.

Ingredients: 6 ounces chicken (white meat)

3 ounces giblets, livers, and kidneys

Sauce of 2 tablespoons *sake*, 2 tablespoons *shoyu*, and 1½ tablespoons sugar

Some powdered ginger or pepper

4 ounces grated Japanese radish (optional)

Preparation: The white meat, giblets, livers, and kidneys of the chicken are cut up into mouthful-size chunks, and spitted alternately on long bamboo skewers. The sauce is prepared and heated separately. The spitted chicken chunks are dipped

83

and roasted over a charcoal or gas flame until browned and roasted. Baste the meats occasionally with the sauce. One may also skewer hard sections of leek or onion, and slices of white or sweet potato, these being cooked in the same way as the chicken.

If the grated radish is used, mix some grated ginger and a dash of the pepper with the radish and roll the cooked chicken chunks in the mixture before eating.

Skewered Shrimp

Another delicious preparation involves lobster, shrimp, or prawns, spitted with pickled lotus root, okra, or asparagus chunks.

Ingredients: 4 large shrimp

A sauce of 1 tablespoon salt, 3½ tablespoons *shoyu*, ¾ tablespoon *sake*, ¼ teaspoon grated ginger.

2 long pieces of lotus or okra root, or 4 top ends of asparagus.

Preparation: The shrimp are carefully washed. Then they are cut up into mouthful-size chunks, dipped into the sauce, spitted, and roasted over the charcoal brazier, much as in the case of the roasted chicken. The hard chunks of vegetables are spitted alternately, after being dipped into the sauce. Grated radish may be served as a condiment but if so, it should be mixed with a sprinkling of grated ginger and a dash of pepper.

Shrimp or Prawns Roasted

Here is a second delectable way of preparing roasted shrimp or prawns.

Ingredients: 4 large shrimp or prawns

A sauce of 1 tablespoon salt, 3½ tablespoons *shoyu*, and ½ tablespoon *sake*

Some powdered ginger or red pepper

2 pieces of okra or 4 top ends of asparagus

Some red pepper, 1½

tablespoons of vinegar,
¼ teaspoon salt, and
¼ teaspoon sugar

Preparation: Boil the shrimp for 5 minutes in salt water, peel, and wash. Cut half-way through and soak the shrimp in the sauce. Broil on a grill over a strong flame and baste occasionally. Sprinkle the shellfish with red pepper or ginger and serve.

Slice the lotus root, okra, or asparagus thinly. Boil for a short time and then drench in cold water. Add the vegetable to a mixture of vinegar, salt, sugar and red pepper and serve with the shrimp or prawns.

Roasted Fish

The Japanese perform taste wonders with all kinds of fish and shellfish, and this—a toasted variety—is no exception.

Ingredients: ¾ pound of white-flesh fish
1 tablespoon salt
4 clams
4 mushrooms, prepared
with ¾ teaspoon salt

4 tablespoons vinegar
Some grated Japanese
   radish
2 leeks
1 ½ teaspoons salt

Preparation: The fish is sectioned, sprinkled with salt, and the clams are partially opened. Mushrooms are washed in salt water and cut into small pieces.

The fish and vegetables are cooked in an earthenware saucer or pan which is placed on top of another utensil that contains heated stones. Place this encased mixture in a roasting oven for 15 minutes.

The cooked preparation is usually served with a side dish of tiny sliced leeks and grated radish, or both, and flavored with the vinegar.

Spitted Sea-Bream

Sea-bream, served with vinegared ginger, is the delight of many a Japanese gourmet.

Ingredients: 4 chunks of sea-bream,
                 seasoned with 1 ³/₄
                 tablespoons salt

87

4 stalks ginger
1 1/2 tablespoons vinegar
3/4 teaspoon salt
4 tablespoons *shoyu* mixed
with grated ginger

Preparation: Fish is scaled, and gills removed. Fish is spitted with head, tail, fins intact, smeared with salt on both sides, and roasted over a strong fire.

While the fish is cooling, the young ginger stalks are stripped and put into the salt and vinegar mixture.

Serve the fish with grated radish, treated ginger, and *shoyu* as condiments.

Spitted Eels

One now turns to another skewered dish, this dealing with what foreigners universally love, though at first their tastes are squeamish.

Ingredients: 1 pound eels
Mixture of 2 tablespoons
sake and 2 3/4 tablespoons *shoyu*

3 1/2 cups *dashi* and stock
made from boiling eels'
heads and bones

Preparation: The eels' heads and bones
are removed. Flesh is stripped, laid open, and cut
in halves. The cut portions are spitted and the heads
and bones mixed with the *dashi* and boiled. The
spitted eels themselves are laid on the grill, skin underneath, and roasted. Hard bamboo skewers that will not
burn are used. Mix the soup, *sake* and *shoyu*.

When eels are browned and crisp, they should be
reversed. The exposed surfaces are painted with the
soup-*shoyu-sake* mixture, and re-roasted several times.

Constant fanning of the spitted meat is necessary
while roasting eels, lest the flesh catch fire from the
dripping grease.

Roasted Thrush or Sparrow

First overcome your scruples, lock up your imagination, and prepare for a real, if unusual, taste-treat,
truly Japanese style.

This is the most unique of the spitted offerings.

Ingredients: 4 small thrushes or spar-

89

rows (head, feet, wings)
A sauce of ³/₄ cup *sake,* ³/₄
cup *shoyu,* and 8 table-
spoons sugar
Powdered Japanese pepper

Preparations: First remove the entrails
and then each bird, complete with head, wings, and
feet, is spitted on a hard bamboo or steel skewer and
broiled lightly over a charcoal brazier. The sauce is
heated independently. The half-cooked birds are
dipped into this sauce several times, each time being
roasted more thoroughly. After they are sprinkled with
Japanese red pepper they are ready to be served.

Tuna Fish & Vegetables Roasted

Tuna or similar fish may be deliciously prepared,
using *shoyu* and *toso* together with vegetables.

Ingredients: 4 pieces tuna or some
similar fish
A sauce of 1 tablespoon
salt, 2¹/₂ tablespoons
shoyu, and 2 ¹/₂ table-
spoons *toso*

> 4 small turnips, cucumbers, or eggplants
>
> Mixture of ³/₄ teaspoon sugar, 1¹/₂ tablespoons vinegar, ³/₄ tablespoon *sake*, and some red pepper

Preparation: Tuna and similar fish are naturally salty so smear very little salt on both sides.

The fish is spitted, broiled until browned, dipped three times into the *shoyu-toso* mixture, and roasted on both sides. Before the third time, the skewers are taken out so that the *shoyu-toso* mixture permeates the insides of the fish.

Vegetables are peeled, diced, and lightly boiled in salt water. When they are quite soft, they are soaked in the suggested mixture of sugar, vinegar, and *sake* for perhaps an hour. Red pepper is sprinkled lightly over these treated vegetables.

A slice of fish is served with a portion of these vegetables.

Some cooks suggest that the broiled fish be soaked for two hours in a *shoyu* sauce and then sprinkled with sesame seed before serving.

Roasted Egg & Fish

Simple but tasty, this takes time to prepare but is well worth the effort.

Ingredients: 3 ounces of white-flesh fish, seasoned with 1/4 teaspoon salt

4 eggs

2 3/4 tablespoons sugar

3 1/2 tablespoons *dashi*

1 1/2 tablespoons *shoyu*

1 1/2 tablespoons *sake*

4 saucers of grated radishes, garnished with 1/4 tablespoon *shoyu* apiece

Preparation: Clean and salt the fish. Carefully remove bones and fish skin, treating the flesh with salt. Using the flat of a knife, mash the fish and rub in the required sugar. Add the beaten eggs, then the *dashi*, *shoyu* and *sake*. Roast the mixture in an earthenware saucepan, which the Japanese call *horoku*.

When browned remove the mixture, laying it

across a bamboo lattice mat. While still hot, the treated fish is rolled tightly in a long roll, using the mat. Left for some time to cool, it is then sliced into half-inch sections. This dish resembles to some extent the *sushi* rice-sandwich, *norimaki-zushi*.

The roll may be served with grated radish, *shoyu*, powdered ginger, and maybe some lemon juice. The eggroll is dipped into this mixture and is eaten.

Roasted Ear Shell

This broiled dish employs turbo sea shells, found abundantly throughout Japan. Uniquely, it is cooked in its own shell.

Ingredients:
- 3 ear shells (turbo)
- 3 dried mushrooms
- A sauce of 1³/₄ tablespoons *dashi*, ¹/₂ teaspoon *shoyu*, and ¹/₂ teaspoon sugar
- 4 chestnuts
- 3 ounces spinach or other leafy vegetable

A second mixture of $1/2$ tablespoon *sake*, $1^1/4$ cups *dashi*, and 5 tablespoons *shoyu*

Preparation: The turbo is broiled in its shell, then cooled. The firm flesh and entrails are scooped out, and the flesh sliced. Vegetables and mushrooms are partially cooked, then they are cut up and added to the shell fish. All are flavored with the sauce of *dashi*, *shoyu*, and sugar. The chestnuts are shelled and mashed.

The four ingredients, turbo, vegetables, treated mushrooms, and chestnuts, are combined with all of these being stuffed back into the ear shell, the open end of which is soaked in the second mixture of *sake*, *shoyu*, and *dashi*. The shell is closed and put back on the fire for rebroiling.

The hard shell-lid which caps the opening is thrown away after cooking.

One may prepare a more tart sauce of vinegar and grated ginger in lieu of the *dashi-shoyu-sake* mixture.

Roasted Vegetables

This odd dish requires fleshy types of vegetables, such as eggplant, carrots, turnips, squash, etc.

Ingredients: 8 to 10 ground-up peanuts
4 tablespoons *dashi*
1³/₄ tablespoons *sake*
2 egg yolks, whipped
1³/₄ tablespoons sugar

Preparation: The sauce is prepared in the following manner—in a pan, add in this order: the peanuts, *dashi*, sugar, *sake*, and the whipped egg yolks. Stir the mixture.

The vegetables one uses are washed, drained, and cut into proper cooking lengths. The vegetables may either be spitted and roasted, or they may be broiled on a grill. In either case, the vegetables are dipped or brushed with the prepared sauce before being cooked.

9

BOILED FOODS

Many Japanese boiled foods, or *nimono* as they are called, bear much resemblance to dinners served in a Cape Cod style. They consist of boiled vegetables, fish, dried fish, and meats, prepared with different and characteristically Oriental sauces made from *shoyu, toso, dashi, miso,* or sugar.

Foremost of the boiled foods are these: boiled shrimp and bamboo shoots; boiled sea-bream with vegetables; boiled chicken, vegetables and eggs; and plain boiled vegetables. These and other tasty recipes will be offered in this chapter.

Shrimp & Bamboo Shoots

This dish combines delicacies of sea and land in a tasty, wine-cooked manner.

Ingredients: 8 shrimp
2 ¹/₂ tablespoons *shoyu*
2 ¹/₂ tablespoons water
1 ¹/₂ tablespoons *mirin*
³/₄ pound bamboo shoots,
fresh or canned

Preparation: First remove the heads and clean the shrimp. Add the *mirin* and *shoyu* to some boiling water and then cook the shrimp in this mixture. Cut the shoots into small sections.

Take out the shrimp and boil the cut-up shoots in the same liquid used for the shrimp. Serve together.

Sea-Bream & Vegetables

Here, among the boiled foods, is the great Japanese delicacy, *tai*, or sea-bream.

Ingredients: 1 medium size *tai*
3 ³/₄ tablespoons *shoyu*
1 ¹/₂ tablespoons *sake*
2 cups water
4 ounces peas
4 ounces cauliflower or
cabbage

Preparation: Remove the fish's head and entrails. The sea-bream is then sliced into three pieces, cut horizontally from the head to the tail. The water is boiled in a pan and the *shoyu* and *sake* added. The fish filets are added to this treated water and allowed to boil for about seven minutes. Diced vegetables are added to the simmering mixture and allowed to cook for about five minutes. All are served at once.

Chicken, Vegetables, & Egg

Here is another tasty example of how the Japanese can successfully combine chicken, eggs, and vegetables.

Ingredients:
2 eggs
6 ounces chicken (white meat)
4 dried mushrooms
1 onion
1 ounce snow peas
Some cooking oil
1 tablespoon *sake*
3 tablespoons sugar
³/₄ teaspoon salt
2 tablespoons *shoyu*
2 ½ tablespoons *dashi*

Preparation: Slice the chicken. Soften the mushrooms in tepid water and slice. Halve and slice the onion. Wash the peas and boil them in salted water. Lightly fry the mushrooms and onion in a mixture of the *dashi*, *sake*, *shoyu*, sugar, and salt. Place the vegetables and sauce of liquid ingredients in a saucepan and lay the chicken slivers on top. Cover the saucepan and boil over a light fire, adding the peas later.

Next, beat the eggs and pour the frothy mixture over the chicken and vegetables while they are boiling. This crusted pie effect of vegetable-chicken-egg is then taken out from the pan and served in four deep bowls. Over each portion is poured a little of the sauce used for cooking

Shrimp, Chicken, & Vegetables

A somewhat fancier mixture including boiled chicken and shrimp and a variety of vegetables, minus the eggs.

Ingredients: 8 ounces chicken (white meat)
3 ³/₄ tablespoons *sake*
³/₄ tablespoon *shoyu*
4 shrimp

¼ teaspoon salt
24 snow peas, seasoned
  with ¼ teaspoon salt
1 pound bamboo shoots
4 dried mushrooms
Mixture of ¾ cup *dashi*,
  3 tablespoons sugar, 2
  tablespoons *shoyu*, and
  ¼ tablespoon salt

Preparation: Boil the shrimp in salted water. Boil again with the mixture of *dashi*, *shoyu*, salt, and sugar. Next boil the peas, once in water and then again in the shrimp liquid. Boil the diced chicken, using the same liquid, but adding the *sake*. The bamboo shoots are next boiled, and again the same liquid is used. The dried mushrooms are softened in tepid water, cut up, and added to the boiling bamboo shoots. Then, all of these boiled ingredients are mixed together and served.

Boiled Vegetables

This is the closest Japanese approximation to a real old-fashioned New England boiled dinner. Not too close perhaps, but both novel and tasty.

Ingredients: 8 ounces beans or peas
3/4 cup *dashi*
1 1/2 tablespoons *shoyu*
1 1/2 tablespoons sugar
2 raw eggs

Preparation: Vegetables are partially boiled with *dashi*, *shoyu*, and sugar. When the vegetables become soft, whip the eggs and pour, in their raw state, over the vegetable mixture. Put the lid on the steaming pot and allow to simmer. Serve hot.

Turbo

Turbo, also called ear shell, may be made into a delicious boiled dish. The shell to be used should be the red-brown, not the bluish type.

Ingredients: 1 turbo
3/4 cup water
2 1/2 tablespoons sugar
2 1/2 tablespoons *shoyu*
3/4 tablespoons *sake*

Preparation: Remove the meat from the shell of the turbo. Place it in a saucepan and boil until soft in just enough water to cover. Add the

JAPANESE FOOD AND COOKING

condiments gradually while the meat is boiling. Reduce the fire to a low boil and allow the treated turbo flesh to simmer. Serve.

Boiled Turnip

This is a simple Japanese favorite.

Ingredients: 1 pound turnips
$^1/_2$ cup sugar
1 $^1/_2$ tablespoons *shoyu*
1 $^1/_4$ teaspoons salt
1 $^1/_2$ cups water

Preparation: Cut the turnip into chunks, without removing the skin. Boil with water and sugar and add the salt and the *shoyu*. Boil until this mixture permeates the turnip. Serve hot.

Sea-Bream Roe & Vegetables

This is a dish which combines green vegetables with delectable sea-bream roe.

Ingredients: 8 ounces sea-bream roe
A sauce of $^3/_4$ cup *dashi*,
$1^1/_4$ tablespoons *shoyu*,
$1^1/_2$ tablespoons *sake*

> and a pinch of salt
> ³/₄ tablespoon sugar (added later)
> Some grated ginger
> 6 ounces vegetables: green peas, celery, and Brussels sprouts
> ¹/₄ teaspoon salt

Preparation: Soak the roe in water for an hour. Take out and cut into inch-long pieces. Mix the *dashi*, the *sake*, the sugar, and the *shoyu*, and bring to a boil. Add slices of ginger or grated ginger while cooking. Sprinkle the roe with the salt.

Then add the sea-bream roe pieces to this boiling mixture and allow to cook until fully saturated and flavored. Remove the roe pieces and boil the vegetables in the same liquid that the roe was cooked in. Flavor with salt to taste. Serve while piping hot.

10

STEAMED DISHES

If the boiled Japanese foods bear some resemblance to dishes served in Boston, Portland, Manchester, and Hartford, the steamed foods which the Japanese call *mushimono* are totally and interestingly different.

This section includes two noted Japanese favorites, the *chawan-mushi* and the *odamaki-mushi*. There are also a number of lesser-known but delectable dishes in this classification.

But let's save the best for last and start off with the less familiar steamed food recipes.

First, though, let us say that there are two chief ways of steaming:

First, one may steam the various ingredients in small bowls and serve in the same bowls that they have been steamed in.

Second, one may steam the food together in one large pan and then serve on individual plates.

Matsutake Dobin

Here is a rare Japanese treat, mushrooms cooked with sauce in a small earthenware pot. *Matsutake* means tree mushrooms and Japan abounds with them. *Dobin* is the small pot used in preparation; it is actually a teapot.

Ingredients: 4 large mushrooms, seasoned with 1 1/2 tablespoon *sake*, 1/4 teaspoon salt

4 ounces chicken (white meat)

4 ounces white-flesh fish

Small bunch watercress

16 gingko nuts or chestnuts

A mixture of 1 cup *dashi*, 3/4 teaspoon salt, and 3/4 tablespoon *shoyu*

3/4 tablespoon fresh lemon juice, added later

Preparation: First one must acquire four *dobin*, one per guest. Each guest also should have a wine cup into which the soup liquid may be poured.

Mushrooms are sliced lengthwise, then cut up and seasoned with the salt and *sake*.

The chicken and white-flesh fish are both cut up and seasoned with the same salt and *sake* mixture from which the mushrooms have temporarily been taken. Watercress is cut up fine.

Parch the gingko or chestnuts and take off the hard outer shell. Cook the nuts in boiling water.

Put the mushrooms, chicken, white-flesh fish, nuts, watercress, and the mixture of *dashi*, *shoyu*, and salt into the four *dobin* to be used. Put each *dobin* on the fire and steam for 20 minutes.

When the *dobin* is served, pour the liquid from the pot into the cup and drink. A side dish of lemon sauce, perhaps with some vinegar added to taste, is served. One may wish to dip the cooked meat, fish, and vegetables into this sauce before eating.

Steamed Ear Shell

Again the tasty turbo, this time steamed with salt.

Ingredients: 2 ear shells (turbo)
Mixture of 1 1/2 cups water,
1 1/4 tablespoons *sake*,
and 1 1/2 teaspoons salt

Another side mixture of
3½ tablespoons *shoyu*
and some grated ginger

Preparation: Always use fresh ear shells, either turbo or abalone. Place these first in a saucepan, without removing the hard outer shell lid. Add water, then add the *sake* and the salt. Boil the whole mixture over a low fire.

Turn the shells over during the boiling. When the sauce is reduced to half, take the saucepan from the fire and remove the lid from the ear shell. Take out the inside flesh, cut it up, and throw away the hard shell.

Serve the ear shell meat and the sauce in which it was cooked in a deep dish. Serve alongside a small dish containing ginger mixed with *shoyu*.

Egg Custard

This employs eggs and the *tofu* that the Japanese and an increasing number of foreigners find so tasty.

Ingredients: 2 eggs
¼ cup *dashi*
½ teaspoon *shoyu*
½ teaspoon salt
4 pieces bean curd

Preparation: Flavor the *dashi* with the *shoyu* and the salt. Heat and then allow it to cool.

Whip the two eggs thoroughly, adding the *dashi* flavoring. Steam in a bowl for 20 minutes, the bowl being already placed inside a steam kettle. The hardened mixture should be sliced and served in a clear soup. This mixture resembles Japanese bean curd. It is equally delicious served hot in winter or cold with ice cubes in summer.

And if one desires, one may add as an extra ingredient, the actual bean curds themselves. Four, one per each guest, are suggested. They may be added with the eggs before the steaming process begins.

Steamed Salt Fish

This is simple to prepare, rewarding to eat.

Ingredients: ³/₄ pound white-flesh fish: sea-bream, cod, halibut, or flounder, seasoned with ³/₄ tablespoon salt

Mixture of 2 tablespoons *shoyu*, ³/₄ tablespoon vinegar, ³/₄ tablespoon lemon juice, and ¹/₄ teaspoon salt.

> 4 ounces Japanese grated
> radish
> 1 leek

Preparation: The fish should be carefully scaled and cleaned, and the head should be removed. Wash the fish well and carefully salt the flesh.

The fish should be set on an earthenware platter and immersed in a large saucepan of boiling water. It is boiled for 20 minutes, then allowed to steam for 10 minutes more. It should be served very hot, with small side dishes of *shoyu*, lemon juice, and vinegar, and other dishes containing grated Japanese radish and thinly sliced Japanese leeks. The fish chunks are dipped into the mixtures before eating.

And now, the great dishes, the *chawan-mushi* and the *odamaki-mushi*.

Chawan-Mushi

Few Japanese dishes are more famous than this custard, either from the native or foreign point of view.

> **Ingredients:** 4 ounces chicken
> 8 shrimp, seasoned with
> $3/4$ cup *shoyu*

24 dried gingko nuts or
chestnuts

4 dried mushrooms

Sauce from 3 cups *dashi*,
$^1/_4$ teaspoon *shoyu*, and
$^1/_4$ teaspoon *sake*

4 eggs, prepared with 2
cups *dashi*, $1^1/_2$ tablespoons *shoyu*, and 1
teaspoon salt

Small bunch of leafy vegetables

Juice of 1 lemon

Preparation: Slice the chicken wafer-
thin to ensure a tender taste after cooking. Remove
head, shell, and entrails of the shrimp. Allow the flesh
to soak for some time in $^3/_4$ cup of *shoyu*.

Parch the shelled nuts and wash carefully.

Stem the mushrooms, soften them, cut them,
and boil them in the sauce of the *dashi*, *sake*, and the
shoyu.

Wash the leafy vegetables and cut into inch long
lengths. Beat the eggs thoroughly, adding the *dashi*,
the *shoyu*, and the salt.

Place all the ingredients except the vegetables in small bowls. Pour over them the whipped eggs, then lay the vegetables on the top of this, thus mingling the chicken, the shrimp, the nuts, and the mushrooms with the mixture of vegetables and eggs in bowls.

Set the bowls in boiling water, letting the water simmer for perhaps 15 minutes until the mixture is hardened in the bowls like custard.

Take the bowls from the steam kettle, put them on plates, and serve each piping hot with a piece of lemon rind on top for flavoring. Over each may be poured a little fresh lemon juice for extra taste.

Odamaki-Mushi

This dish—steamed noodles, fish roll, eggs, and vegetables—is just about as simple to make, as the preceeding dish, once proper care has been taken. Constant surveillance and attention is needed here no less than in the preparation of the *chawan-mushi*.

Ingredients: 1½ cups boiled macaroni or vermicelli, seasoned with ¾ tablespoon *shoyu*

1 roll of fish paste
1 slice of ham
3 mushrooms
Small handful of leafy vegetables
Sauce from 4 eggs, 2 cups
dashi, 1/2 teaspoon *sake*,
1 1/2 tablespoons *shoyu*,
and 1/2 teaspoon salt

Preparation: The *udon* or macaroni is
first boiled, then mixed with the *shoyu*. The fish paste
and the ham are sliced into 1/4 inch thicknesses. Mushrooms are set in water to soften and then cut up. Leafy
vegetables are also softened and cut up.

Next, the eggs are beaten and mixed with the *dashi*,
the *sake*, the *shoyu*, and the salt.

Put the boiled noodles into four small bowls and
add the mushrooms, the fish paste, the ham, and the
leafy vegetables. Over everything pour the egg sauce.

This whole mixture is then steamed in a large
steam kettle for about 20 minutes. The bowls are then
placed on plates and served individually. Lemon juice
may be added if desired, poured over the hot custard.

II
FRIED FOODS

This is the Japanese equivalent of the American southern fried favorites, and has already been partly introduced with the mention of *tendon* and *tempura* in chapter two.

This text may thus pass over *tempura* and proceed to the second fried-foods category, or *agemono*, which the Japanese call *karaage*-style.

This word comes from two Japanese ideographs: *kara* meaning empty and *age* meaning to fry. Emptily (perhaps lightly or hollowly) fried would seem to be the meaning.

Karaage consists of fish, meat, or vegetables fried with little oil and without the batter coating we know so well from the *tempura* preparations. Frying is done after putting some cornstarch only over the ingredients. Otherwise, the same things are used as in the case of the *tempura*.

Three recipes mentioned here demonstrate amply

that the *tempura* style is by no means confined to lobster, shrimp, or prawn.

Fresh Shrimp & Vegetables

This is of course definitely in the *tempura* class and is just about as delicious.

Ingredients: 8 shrimp
$1^1/_2$ ounces onions
$1^1/_2$ ounces carrots
$^3/_4$ cup flour
4 tablespoons water
$1^1/_2$ cup sesame oil
4 ounces grated radish
Sauce from $^1/_2$ cup *dashi*,
2 tablespoons *shoyu*,
and $^1/_2$ tablespoon sugar

Preparation: First, remove the head and the outer shell of the shrimp or prawns used. Then, two at a time, roll these in the flour and water batter. Cut up the onions next and slice the carrots and dip these into the batter. All ingredients must be dry before dipping.

Heat the sesame oil and fry the shrimp in it, then fry the treated vegetables. Mix the *dashi* with the *shoyu* and the sugar, add one tablespoon of grated Japanese radish, and used this sauce as a dip for the fried foods.

Grated ginger may be added for extra flavoring.

Tablefish *Tempura*

Fish, such as mackerel, cod, flounder, etc. may be served *tempura*-style with marked success.

Ingredients: 2 fish, 4 ounces apiece, seasoned with $^3/_4$ teaspoon salt and $^1/_4$ teaspoon pepper

$2^1/_2$ tablespoons cornstarch, mixed with water

$1 ^1/_2$ cups sesame seed oil

$^1/_2$ cucumber

Sauce prepared from $1 ^1/_2$ tablespoons vinegar or lemon juice, $^1/_4$ tablespoon grated ginger, and 2 tablespoons *shoyu*.

Preparation: Remove the head and entrails of the fish, cut the remainder lengthwise but not through. Sprinkle the fish flesh with the salt and pepper.

Make a paste from the cornstarch and the water. Dip the fish into this mixture and then fry in the sesame or the other vegetable cooking oil used. Cut the half cucumber into inch-long strips and add salt. The fish is served with the cucumber as a garnish.

A tart sauce is prepared from the vinegar, *shoyu*, and grated Japanese ginger, and the fish chunks are dipped into this before eating.

Vegetable *Tempura*

This is a style where all the vegetables to be used are dipped into a *tempura* batter and served piping hot, *tempura*-style.

The vegetables recommended for this unique " southern-fried" treatment are as follows: eggplant, carrots, burdock, onion leek, or any kind of potato, sweet or white.

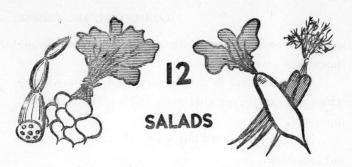

12

SALADS

One major difference of interest to note is that, while foreigners in the West prepare their salads entirely of raw ingredients, the salads of the Japanese are almost entirely vegetables that have been cooked in advance—perhaps as a precautionary health measure.

The Japanese are great salad eaters. There are two main types of salads : *tsukemono*, literally pickled vegetables ; and *sunomono*, or vinegared dishes. Both of these are served with the many distinct types of *aemono*, or salad dressings.

These dishes are eaten, just as in the Western world, after the main course, after the final course, even ahead of the meal, or with *sake* as a sort of appetizer or *hors d'oeuvre*. These latter two ways of course are in the Oriental, not the Occidental tradition.

Often the vinegared dishes are eaten beforehand, usually with the heated *sake*. These usually consist of fresh, raw, or boiled vegetables, fish or shellfish, and are flavored with vinegar, *shoyu*, salt, sugar, and sometimes with *sake* itself.

The *tsukemono* is chiefly composed of root vegetables and greens, pickled with salt and bran, or just plain salt.

However, the best-known type is pickled with both salt and bran.

Dried giant white radishes, which the Japanese call *daikon*, are put into large casks with both salt and the bran. These radishes are pressed by a large flat stone for a very long time. Salt bran for this pickling is kept in a cask or jar in each home and restaurant. Root vegetables, greens, eggplant, and cucumbers are other kinds that may be so treated.

The second method employs plain salt. Vegetables are pressed in a cask or an earthenware jar, again by a heavy stone, from several hours to several days, after a liberal sprinkling of salt. Vegetables then are combined with a fermented bean-paste mixture, wine-dregs, or even strong mustard, and again pickled with a good quantity of table salt.

Vegetables do not, however, change their fundamental taste even after lengthy pickling, and yet a vegetable pickled for more than a few days soon has its own distinctive taste and aroma.

Pickled vegetables are always served in a large bowl, attractively arranged.

Japanese chefs recommend the following vegetables as suitable for delicious pickling recipes: carrots, cabbage, radish, turnips, spinach, eggplant, lettuce, and cucumber. Here are some of the recommended salad recipes.

Chinese Lettuce

Japanese have accepted many dishes used originally by the Chinese. This is one of the favorites and is known as *o-shinko*.

Ingredients:	20 pounds of the Chinese lettuce (*hakusai*)
	12 ounces salt
	40-pound stone
	1 large earthenware jar or cask

Preparation: In the first place, let it be mentioned that the Japanese usually prepare this *o-shinko* in bulk for many, many servings.

Cut the Chinese lettuce into halves, then quarters. Wash all of it carefully.

Put some salt into a jar and then put the lettuce

119

flat on the bottom, sprinkling all leaves liberally with salt. Continue to do this until all the leaves have been inserted flatly into the cask. When the container is filled place the heavy stone on top of the leaves. Fill the cask half full of water.

The trick is to wait for pickling, and this is achieved after the water has risen. In summer time, the process takes six to eight hours; in the fall, a day; and in winter, from two to three days. Pickled vegetables are then served with *shoyu*.

Other vegetables such as turnips, greens, spinach, etc. may be similarly pickled and prepared.

Pickled Radish

The other major Japanese salad is pickled, sliced Japanese radish, called *takuan* in Japanese.

Containing a high percentage of diastase, the radish, or *daikon*, is such a good digestive agent that it is one of the vital greens for a rice-eating people. A Japanese saying suggests that no matter how much one overeats boiled rice, some raw radish will quickly settle the stomach.

Of all the many ways of preparing radish, the most popular perhaps is this *takuan* way. This is a radish preserved in rice-bran, and it is eaten throughout the year. The technical name is *takuanzuke*, named for Priest Takuan who invented it to please his Buddhist vegetarian appetite.

According to the priest's way, the radish is first dried in the sun, then preserved in a rice-bran and salt mixture, again by using a cask and the heavy stone. Legend is that the pickle was named because the heavy stone used in pressing looked like the gravestone on Priest Takuan's Tokyo tomb.

A slight variant from this is what the Japanese call *asazuke*, another pickle formed from radish preserved in salt and malt and then fermented.

There are many large radish types, named after the places of their growth, such as: *Nerima-daikon, Sakura-jima-daikon, Kameido-daikon, Moriguchi-daikon*, etc. These species, full-grown, reach four to five feet in length, one to two feet in circumference, and weigh 25 to 40 pounds. Truly an amazing vegetable!

Takuanzuke

This delicious pickle, named after the good priest, is liked even by foreigners.

Ingredients: 16 ounces radish (turnip,

cabbage, cucumber may
also be used but prefer-
ably giant radish)

1½ tablespoons salt

1 stone, twice as heavy
as the radish

1 large receptacle

Preparation: First soak the Japanese radish in a weak solution of bleaching powder, then wash well.

Chop the highly edible leaves, then sprinkle them with salt, rubbing this salt well into the greens. Put these leaves into the cask with a fitted lid smaller than the cask and weight this lid down with the rock. The radish, cut to strips, has of course been added to the leaves inside the cask.

After four to five hours pickling is finished. Serve the leaves and radish strips with *shoyu* and flavor with vinegar, chopped ginger, some red pepper, and maybe a dash of lemon juice.

Next, let us proceed to the five chief types of dressing for salads: (1) *miso*, the fermented bean paste, seasoned with sugar and vinegar; (2) sesame and *shoyu*, seasoned with sugar; (3) sesame and sugar; (4) bean curd, *shoyu*, sugar, and salt and (5) sesame, salt, *shoyu*, vinegar, and sugar.

Any of the vegetables or fish used is boiled, then mixed with one of these types of dressings, and served.

A word about sesame seed. It is usually easy to obtain locally, but if such is not the case, there are several good substitutes available. Ground peanuts or walnuts are a fine substitute. These seeds are ground with a mortar and pestle, crushed and turned into a powder.

And now to list some recipes still belonging to the salads but treated with the Japanese dressings.

Spinach

An outstanding Japanese salad favorite is just plain old spinach, dressed with sesame deeds.

Ingredients: ³/₄ pound fresh spinach
2 tablespoons black or white sesame seeds
2 tablespoons *shoyu*

Preparation: Boil some water in a large saucepan, then put in the spinach which has been cut into inch lengths and thoroughly washed. Boil for three minutes.

The sesame seeds are parched in a frying pan. then ground by the mortar-and-pestle method and, with *shoyu* added, re-ground.

The spinach is then mixed with the sesame dressing and the *shoyu* and served in small saucers.

Vegetables, White Sesame, & Vinegar

Perhaps these are not salads the American housewife usually dishes up, but they are tasty if one follows the preparations with care.

Ingredients:
- 3/4 pound Japanese radish
- 1/4 pound carrots
- 3/4 tablespoon salt (for the above vegetables)
- 1 *aburaage*, a kind of fried Japanese bean curd
- 1 packet of *shirataki*, a kind of Japanese vermicelli, with 1/4 teaspoon salt
- 4 dried mushrooms, sea-

soned with ¼ cup *dashi*,
¾ tablespoon sugar, and
¾ tablespoon *shoyu*
3 tablespoons white sesame
seeds, prepared with 2
tablespoons vinegar, 2
tablespoons sugar, ¾
tablespoon *shoyu*, and
1½ teaspoons salt

Preparation: The radish and carrots are sliced thin. The salt is sprinkled lightly over their tops. The Japanese vermicelli is also rubbed with the salt and cut across three times.

The fried bean curd, the vermicelli, and the de-stalked mushrooms are boiled in the mixture of *dashi*, sugar, and *shoyu*. The Japanese radish and the carrots, already sliced fine, are also boiled in hot water for a short time separately. Afterwards, the water is pressed out.

The white sesame seeds are parched, ground, and flavored with the vinegar, the *shoyu*, the sugar, and the salt. All of these ingredients are then combined and served individually in small bowls.

Small Clams and Onions

This is recommended to all seafood lovers and is unusual both in appearance and taste.

Ingredients: ³/₄ cup small clams

³/₄ pound small onions, or *rakyo* (pickled onions)

Sauce composed of 4 tablespoons *miso*, 2 tablespoons sugar, 2 tablespoons *dashi*, and 2 tablespoons vinegar

Preparation: Instead of clams, of course other types of seafood may be used. These include scallops, shell ligaments, mussels, etc. One may even use such fish as mackerel, tuna, sardines, etc. Canned fish too is a possibility though fresh is better. Whatever is used should first be sprinkled with salt and then soaked in vinegar. The clams, if used, however, require no salt since they have a natural abundance. The onions are sliced and boiled.

To the strained fermented bean paste, add the sugar, the *dashi*, and, after stirring, the vinegar.

The small clams and the onions are then mixed

with this hot *miso* combination and served individually.

Carrots & Kidney Beans

This is a third example of the rather unique way that the Japanese prepare their salad dishes. It is also interestingly delicious.

Ingredients: 1 carrot
24 red kidney beans
$1/4$ teaspoon salt
$1/4$ cup *dashi*
$3/4$ tablespoon sugar
3 tablespoons white sesame seeds
6 ounces bean curd, seasoned with 3 tablespoons sugar, $3/4$ teaspoon salt, and $3/4$ teaspoon *shoyu*

Preparation: The carrot is sliced into thin lengths and these, together with the beans, are sprinkled with salt. Boil slowly and then, after boiling, flavor with the sugar, the *dashi*, and the *shoyu*.

The sesame seeds are parched and the sugar is added.

The bean curd is boiled, all the water is pressed out lightly, and the salt, sugar, and *shoyu* are added and mixed. This is next combined with both the carrots and the red kidney beans and served.

The last part in this salad section deals primarily with what the Japanese know as *sunomono*, or vinegared dishes.

Some are prepared with equal amounts of vinegar and *shoyu* and some with vinegar, *shoyu*, and sugar in thirds.

In this group are some excellent vinegared shellfish dishes; Japanese, fond of shellfish, have seen to that.

Vinegared Scallops or Clams

This may be for a special type of gourmet but it's worth experimenting with. You may not like it, but then again, you may.

Ingredients: 4 scallops or 24 clams
1 1/2 tablespoons vinegar
1 cucumber, seasoned with
1/4 teaspoon salt and
1 1/4 tablespoons vinegar

Sauce composed of 2 tablespoons vinegar or lemon
juice, ¹/₂ teaspoon *sho-
yu*, 3 tablespoons *sake*,
and ³/₄ tablespoon sugar

Preparation: The sea-scallops, or clams
must be cleaned and carefully washed. Their meat is
sliced thin and soaked in the vinegar. Then it is
served in small bowls. The shellfish may be served
either raw, boiled, or steamed.

Slice the cucumber thin from end to end and
sprinkle with salt and vinegar. Let the strips stand for
some time in this vinegar, and then serve with the sea-
scallops or small clams. Over this mixture pour the
sauce of the vinegar, the *shoyu*, the *sake*, and the sugar.

Vinegared Mackerel

Here is an old American favorite, dressed up in a
new way, a special Oriental treatment that foreign diners should enjoy.

Ingredients: 1 pound mackerel
³/₄ cup vinegar
³/₄ tablespoon salt
8 ounces grated radish

Some grated ginger
4 tablespoons fresh lemon
juice or vinegar
1 1/4 teaspoons salt
1/2 teaspoon *shoyu*

Preparation: The fish is scaled and skinned. The entrails are then taken out and the flesh washed, salted, and cut into four slices, one per guest. This flesh is allowed to stand in salt and vinegar for three hours.

Sliced thin, the fish is served individually with a side dish of grated radish, seasoned with powdered ginger, vinegar, *shoyu*, and just a pinch of salt. The fish is dipped into this mixture before eating.

Japanese guests like their strips served raw; however, foreigners sometimes prefer it boiled or steamed. If steamed, be sure and do so before the fish is allowed to sit three hours in the salt and vinegar mixture.

Vinegared Vegetables

Vegetables, especially mushrooms, lend themselves well to the vinegar method of Japanese salad-making.

Ingredients: 8 ounces mushrooms

6 ounces turnips

Sauce made from $1/2$ teaspoon salt, $1/2$ teaspoon *shoyu*, 2 tablespoons *sake*, 2 tablespoons *dashi*, and 2 tablespoons lemon juice

$1 1/2$ tablespoons *katsuobushi* shavings

Preparation: The mushrooms are stemmed and roasted on long metal skewers. Small turnips are boiled until soft and cooled. Turnip greens are cut into inch lengths and the roots are also sliced.

Mushrooms and turnips are served in small individual bowls, each being filled with a mixture of salt, *shoyu*, vinegar, *sake*, and *dashi*. The lemon juice and the shavings are then added to complete the recipe.

Vinegared Turbo

By now the foreign cook should know all about the Japanese ear shell. Here it is in a tasty salad.

Ingredients: $3/4$ pound turbo

1 fresh peach or apple
1 beet or turnip
1/4 teaspoon salt
Sauce from 4 tablespoons
vinegar or fresh lemon
juice, 1 1/2 teaspoons *shoyu*, 1 1/2 teaspoons salt,
4 ice cubes

Preparation: These shells should be green. After careful washing, the shell and flesh are separated, entrails removed, and inner flesh diced and served in medium-size bowls. To this may be added two pieces of fruit or two of vegetables. Then add a little salt water (1/2 cup of water to 1/4 teaspoon salt) and the ice cubes. Over all is poured the sauce.

Vinegared Lobster, Shrimp, or Prawns

Even the King of the Sea can be Japanified. This change, though, only adds to the essential taste appeal.

Ingredients: 3 ounces shrimp, prawns, or lobster, seasoned with 1/2 teaspoon salt, 1 1/2 tablespoons sweet *sake*

4 small cucumbers, seasoned with ³/₄ tablespoon
salt

Sauce made from 2 egg
yolks, ³/₄ tablespoon su-
gar, ¹/₄ teaspoon salt,
1¹/₂ tablespoons vine-
gar, and ¹/₂ tablespoon
sweet *sake*

Preparation: Remove head, shell, and
entrails of seafood used. Wash the meat in salted water,
then lightly boil. Cut into pieces and allow it to stand
in the rice wine.

Slice the cucumbers into inch-lengths. Peel off
the hard outer rind and take out the seedy center part.
Combine the seasoned meat and the cucumbers, sprinkle
with salt, and set aside.

Boil two eggs for 15 minutes. Using only the yolks,
mash these and mix them with the vinegar, the sweet
sake, the sugar, and the salt. The shell-fish and cucumbers may be rolled in the treated egg yolk and eaten,
or they may be eaten separately.

Shoyu Spinach

This recipe book should certainly mention what the Japanese call *hitashimono*, which is boiled greens dipped in *shoyu*, as this is one of the Japanese favorites.

> **Ingredients:** ³/₄ pound spinach
> 4 tablespoons *katsuobushi* shavings
> Sauce made from ¹/₈ cup *dashi* and ¹/₈ cup *shoyu*

Preparation: Boil and then chill the spinach. Cut it into inch-long lengths. Next boil the *dashi* and add the *shoyu*. Let the mixture cool.

Serve the spinach in flat saucers with the green-leaf part and the red-stalk part arranged alternately. Pour the cooled soup-stock mixture over the spinach and sprinkle the shavings over the top. Still another way of serving would be to roll the boiled spinach with dry seaweed or in chopped egg, with a heavy coating of either parched sesame or caraway seeds.

Turnips in *Shoyu*

Several other vegetables may be similarly treated: Chinese cabbage; iceberg lettuce; the fragrant Japanese green, *shungiku*; spinach; but above all, turnips.

Ingredients: ³/₄ pound turnips
Mixture of ¹/₈ cup *dashi*
and ¹/₈ cup *shoyu*

Preparation: First strip the leaves. Next immerse the tubular parts in water and boil slowly. When the tubular parts are soft, the leaves should be dipped in the same water and taken out when the soft steam rises, and then plunged into cold water. The stems and leaves are cut into inch lengths. Both are served in the mixture of the *shoyu* and the soup stock.

13
NOODLES

The Japanese people, as we have seen, require rice as their staple food. But next to rice in importance is what the Italians call *pasta*—noodles, spaghetti, macaroni. Noodle-eating in homes, restaurants, or streetstalls is a part of the national tradition. They may be eaten at any time—breakfast, lunch, dinner, in-between, or served to an unexpected guest.

There are various kinds of noodles—a fat one known as *udon*; a slender green one called *soba* which was originally made in Niigata prefecture, and which is always made from buckwheat flour. *Soba* may also mean Chinese noodles, usually slender ones. All of these may be served in soup, like a sort of stew, or boiled and fried; hot or cold; bland or pungent. At snack time, a bowl of *soba*, soft fried, for example, just hits the spot.

One additional refinement has been added—noodles may be and usually are—served ice cold in the summer.

The green noodles are traditionally served this way. The contrast between the green noodles on the yellow mat, with variously colored garnishes is most appetizing, and helps to make one feel cool.

Kake and *mori* are two words that mean a lot to the *soba* trade. These are the most customary methods of serving noodles. *Kake* refers to the Japanese verb meaning to pour over, since in this way hot soup is poured over the noodles. The word *mori* refers to buckwheat noodles served on a steaming bamboo lattice, known in Japan as *seiro*. The buckwheat noodles are heaped up on this lattice and eaten. *Mori*, the Japanese verb to amass or collect, obviously refers to this method of serving. Again, a bowl of soup accompanies the noodles.

Soba is served in many fashions; such as *okame soba*, which contains mashed fish, mushrooms, and other small flavoring vegetables; *yubasoba*, which serves the dried bean curd in accompaniment; *gomokusoba*, a five-colored variety of the buckwheat noodle, which contains mashed fish, shellfish, egg yolks, and taro root mashed; and *kamonanban*, which contains a few slices of duck meat. Beef or pork, however, may be used just as well.

It isn't at all unusual, even in Tokyo, for a person

137

moving from one place to another to be presented buckwheat noodles by his neighbors. He says at this time, according to Japanese custom, "Three across the street and two on both sides," this as a token of newly-established friendly relations. This comes from the fact that a second reading of the word *soba* may be translated "beside" or "close to," implying a close harmony or near relationship.

On New Year's Eve Japanese eat buckwheat noodles traditionally known as *toshikoshisoba*, or "year-crossing buckwheat noodles." The noodles eaten at this time are said to award the diner special good luck for the new year.

There are two other types of noodles that are commonly eaten in Japan. These are called *somen*, a kind of wheat vermicelli ; and *udon*, also of wheat and called the Japanese macaroni.

All three of these noodle forms may be bought in any neighboring store precooked and ready for heating and eating, or they may be bought in their original dry form and prepared similarly to ordinary macaroni or spaghetti.

There are many and varied recipes for the various *soba*, *udon*, and *somen* dishes, the range being perhaps the greatest with respect to the soba.

In general, one person can be expected to eat about $1/4$ of a pound of one or the other, served with perhaps $1/4$ pound of meat, pork, or chicken strips, and perhaps $1/4$ pound of such vegetables as mushrooms, sweet green peas, cabbage, Chinese cabbage, cooked lettuce, carrots, burdock, leeks, or onion slivers.

The sauce is strictly Chinese, though due to circumstances, it is being adapted more to the use of Japanese, not Chinese, ingredients.

Strictly speaking, this is a variety of food imported from China and as such does not come within the scope of this book. It is mentioned indeed since the Japanese themselves are such inveterate noodle-eaters.

One final word on noodle-eating in general. The Japanese are under no such restraint in noisy eating as are the average foreigners. *Soba*, *udon*, and *somen* are all slurped or at least loudly sucked.

14
DESSERTS

Foreigners may not think of desserts in Japan except in terms of the pies, cakes, and ice creams usually available in the Western-style restaurants. But he should investigate further and see the rich variety of Japanese cakes and biscuits awaiting his approval.

Dessert in one word might be spelled *o-kashi*, the Japanese word for cake(s).

These cakes employ purely native materials, combined in an essentially Japanese fashion to make results that are equally attractive to the sight, the smell, and the taste.

Japanese cakes are made from such ingredients as red beans, rice, agar-agar or gelatine, rice flour, corn flour or cornstarch, bean flour or potato starch (including sweet potatoes), eggs, sugar, millet jelly, and some lesser materials. Aromatics and colorings also play their part.

There are mainly two kinds of desserts—the dry

confectionery and the cakes. The first category would consist of such Japanese specialties as rice or corn-flour wafers, and candied sweets made from millet jelly, sugar, and wheat gluten.

The cakes may be broken down into those made from red, black, or green bean paste; sugar and Japanese isinglass; sweet buns filled with bean paste, sugar, rice or wheat, corn-flour or starch; hard rice biscuits, browned and served in various shapes; cakes with seaweed strips, baked and then painted with *shoyu*; and cakes that taste like lumps of colored sugar.

In all cases, the ingredients are always quite simple to find throughout the year and in every part of the country.

Rice Wafers

These rice cakes, which the Japanese call *o-sembei*, are perhaps the cheapest native confections.

Rice or wheat flour is kneaded into a dough. This is mixed with egg yolk, seaweed, sesame seed, corn or cornstarch, and certain spices. The mixture is baked in a thin metal mold.

According to the materials used, this rice wafer may be sub-divided into *tamago-sembei* (egg); *nori-sembei* (seaweed); *ebi-sembei* (shrimp or prawns baked with the original dough); *kani-sembei* (crab); *goma-sembei* (sesame seed); and *tomorokoshi-sembei* (corn).

Sembei are named often after their assumed shapes, i.e.: *kame-no-ko sembei* (tortoise child); *kawara-sembei* (roof-tile); *kiraku-sembei* (light-hearted wafers); *Isobe-sembei* (from Isobe, a famous hot spring resort town); *shio-sembei* (salt); and the *tsujiura-sembei* (containing good fortune slips baked in with the dough).

There are several other noted kinds: *Chuka-sembei* (named after a great Japanese geographer who drew Japan's first really modern maps and whose likeness appears stamped on each rice wafer); *imo-sembei* (sweet potato mix); *taru-sembei* (barrel-shaped); *Kamakura-kawara sembei* (resembling the old roof tiles of this ancient Japanese capital city); *kikusui-sembei* (crysanthemum-wafer, denoting a noted family's house crest); and, of course, the celebrated *Heiji-sembei* (baked in the shape of a rice farmer's straw hat). This one has a fascinating story.

Heiji was a poor warrior, a descendant of the noble Taira clan which was virtually decimated in the 11th century battle of Dan-no-Ura with the rival Genji clan. Unable to buy fish for his old mother, Heiji traveled to Akogi-no-Ura, a fish preserve where fish to be offered at the Ise Grand Shrine were kept until needed.

This warrior, while stealing some fish, was seized

and arrested. Fleeing, he abandoned his straw hat, on the brim of which were written the two characters of his name, Hei and Ji. He was arrested and brought to trial.

An oted man, one Hirakawa Jirozo, had been under a deep moral debt to this Heiji. To discharge this debt, he himself appeared before the court, declaring Heiji's innocence, claiming the hat as his own, and insisting the characters on Heiji's hat were his own.

Heiji accordingly was set free and the noble Hirakawa took his place in jail.

The rice cake flourished from then on, always fashioned in the shape of the celebrated and abandoned straw hat.

Now, back to the Japanese cakes.

Ingredients are simple, cheap, and easy to find. There are varieties of kinds, shapes, and colors, and the differences come from the combination of ingredients and the way in which they are prepared.

The chief ingredient is usually either paste made from mashed potatoes or from mashed beans, these being boiled with sugar, isinglass, seaweed, and sometimes *sake*.

To make bean paste use two cups of red kidney beans, 2 cups of sugar, and 2 tablespoons of salt.

For the strained paste, the housewife will first wash the beans, then boil them. The water should generously cover the beans. Then boil until the shells are broken and the beans become soft.

These beans are strained, put into a coarse cotton bag, and the water is squeezed out. The sugar is added bit by bit. Salt is next added to the strained beans and these are then boiled over a low flame, stirring constantly.

The mashed bean paste is similarly prepared. First add sugar and some salt to the soft, boiled red beans, letting this mixture boil down.

Potato paste is similarly prepared. Using either the new or the sweet potatoes, they are boiled, strained free of water, and reboiled with the sugar and the salt added.

Agar-agar, or what the Japanese call *kanten*, is another key ingredient.

Soak this gelatinous substance in water, using $1\frac{1}{2}$ times as much water as agar-agar. After some time, when it has expanded, boil it until it melts. Next strain and cool, then add sugar, bean paste, egg whites, and sometimes even fruit juices, together with aromatics and coloring.

The agar-agar itself congeals at about 85 degrees F. The housewives must take care to add the egg whites and the bean paste after the agar-agar liquid has become cold or else the ingredients may separate from one another.

This agar-agar is like a gelatin, but it is hailed as being better for usual kitchen purposes than gelatin because it does not melt even though the air outside, as in summer, is excessively hot.

Now, we can proceed to a more detailed analysis of the main types of Japanese cakes.

Red Bean Cake

This is a kind of bean paste candy, often served alone with tea, and a favorite of adult and child alike.

Ingredients: Agar-agar, one cake
2 cups water
Bean paste, made from 2 cups red kidney beans, 2 cups sugar, and 2 tablespoons salt
2 cups white sugar
2 tablespoons millet jelly
1 egg white

Preparation: Boil the agar-agar with water. Add and melt the sugar. Strain carefully.

Put the saucepan over the fire again and add, in turn, the salt, the bean paste, the egg white, and the millet jelly. Stir carefully, as if kneading. Boil the mixture down into a gluey, starchy residue and, while still liquid, pour into a square metal mold and allow to cool. Cut the molded substance into rectangles about two inches long and one inch wide.

Specialists suggest that in summer one more cup of water and ½ teaspoon of salt be added. This red bean cake, *yokan* to the Japanese, may be served after being cooled with ice cubes.

White-of-Egg Cake

Not too different from the red bean cake but different enough is this dessert-type delicacy.

Ingredients: Agar-agar
2 cups water
2 cups sugar
2 tablespoons millet jelly
1 egg white

Preparation: First, melt the agar-agar as usual and add the sugar. Then strain. Put the saucepan with the strained, sugared agar-agar back over the fire and add the millet jelly gradually before reboiling.

146

Continue the boiling until the mixture hangs down in threads when held in the air. Take off the fire entirely and let the mixture cool.

Beat the egg white thoroughly, adding little by little the cooled agar-agar mixture. Then pour this mixture into the metal mould. When it has congealed remove the paste from the mould and cut into the usual rectangles. The Japanese call this *awayukikan*.

Bean & Jam Bun

This sweet is served with a crust mixed with powdered Japanese green ceremonial tea. It is unusual and, many say, delicious.

Ingredients: 2 cups sugar
3 cups flour
1 teaspoon green ceremonial powdered tea
1 cup water
2 cups strained bean paste

Preparation: First place the sugar in a bowl containing one cup of water. Dissolve. Sift the flour and then sift the powdered tea, to remove all lumps. Add both of these to the sugared water, making

147

a paste which is then formed into small round sheets.

Divide the bean paste into small balls. Wrap them in the small sheets of dough, like a filled dumpling.

Finally, spread a wet cloth, the hand towel that Japanese call *o-shibori*, over the buns. Steam them inside this towel over a strong fire for maybe a quarter of an hour.

Red Kidney Bean Soup Cake

This is actually a soup combined with a dumpling. The Japanese, known to favor this immensely, call it *shiruko*.

Ingredients: 2 cups red kidney beans
2 cups sugar
$1/2$ teaspoon salt
1 tablespoon arrowroot starch
3 cups water
6-8 pieces of rice cake

Preparation: Make the bean paste in the usual way with the red beans, the sugar, and the salt. Add this paste to boiling water. Separately the arrowroot starch is dissolved in very hot water and then added to the bean soup. This will thicken the overall mixture.

Toast the rice cakes gently. Place them in the separate bowls, one, perhaps two, depending on the size of the bowl. Pour over these cakes or dumplings the hot bean soup and serve.

Sweet Potato Paste Cake

This unusual dessert is simply potato paste shaped in a small face. or hand-towel, an *o-shibori*.

Ingredients: 6 cups strained boiled sweet
potatoes
2 cups white sugar
1 ½ teaspoons salt
Some boiled or fresh sweet
fruit or chestnuts

Preparation: First, cut the fruit to be used into very small pieces.

Next, mix the strained sweet potatoes with both sugar and salt. Knead together over a slow fire.

Place some of this flavored potato mixture on a dry face towel and mix it with some of the fruit pieces. Place the towel in the left hand, turning it around,

149

twisting it with the right hand to give the inner fruit and potato mixture an odd, twisted appearance. Take off the face towel and serve the odd shape, generally two or three per guest.

This cake has an odd Japanese name. It is called the *chakin shibori*.

Bean & Jam Cake

Last in the sweet-tooth section is this cake, also of bean jam, wrapped in an arrowroot crust.

Ingredients: 1 cup arrowroot starch
1 ½ cups white sugar
3 cups water
3 cups strained bean paste
Green leaves for decoration

Preparation: Add the starch to the water and the sugar and boil until it becomes clear, even a little sticky. Take the saucepan from the fire, putting on a lid to prevent it from cooling. Mold the strained bean paste into the required number of balls, two per guest, or perhaps three.

Next, transfer enough of the arrowroot liquid to a large serving bowl so as to half fill it. Place in this bowl a bean-paste ball, this of course quite naturally sinking to the bottom. This ball will then be coated with the arrowroot liquid.

Shape each ball so treated, wrapping it around with a green leaf for decoration. Steam for 15 minutes. Cool and then serve.

Again, as with the red bean paste cake, place ice cubes around the balls for summer servings.

Japanese know this cake as *kuzumanju.*

15

FESTIVAL DISHES

Every Japanese loves a festival and, what's more, he loves the food that is traditionally served with it. There are many dishes, some quite simple, some very exotic, but not all of them would tickle the foreigners fancy as they do the Japanese.

However, it does not seem amiss to include mention of some of these dishes in the belief that preparation will be interesting and that the result may be considered tasty.

New Year's is of course the outstanding Japanese holiday, an occasion that goes on for five to six days and which is replete with various time-honored dishes.

Lobster, fish, soup, cakes, special vegetables, and traditionally prepared *sake* all play their part in these festival feasts.

Lobster

Used in practically any season, this King of the Sea, in Japan as elsewhere, finds himself put to special holiday uses.

152

Ingredients: 3 medium-size prawns, shrimp or lobster
1 tablespoon *mirin*
5 tablespoons *shoyu*
$^1/_4$ to $^1/_2$ teaspoon powdered Japanese pepper

Preparation: The seafood used is boiled for 10 minutes in salt water, then cooled. Legs, antenna, head, and tail are cut off. Entrails are removed. Cut halfway through the shrimp, lobster, or prawns and fill with the mixture of sweet *mirin* and *shoyu*. Broil on a grill some distance from a strong fire. This process of insertion and broiling is repeated several times. The shellfish is sprinkled with red pepper and served on a large platter.

Turnips

This simple little vegetable can be dressed up for the special holiday occasion.

Ingredients: 4 small turnips
A sauce of $^3/_4$ tablespoon vinegar, $^1/_4$ tablespoon white sugar, $^3/_4$ tablespoon *mirin*, and 1 $^1/_4$ teaspoons salt

153

Preparation: Peel the turnips. Cut them lengthwise twice at 90° angles without cutting all the way through. Sprinkle salt over them and then boil lightly. When properly softened, soak the turnips in the vinegar, sugar, salt, and *mirin* for perhaps an hour. The red pepper is chopped up. Some pieces are put in the middle of the sliced turnips, making the turnips resemble a chrysanthemum.

Sweet Soy Beans

Exotic treatment awaits these plain old beans in this special seasonal dish, a treat for foreigners no less than Japanese.

> **Ingredients**: 1 cup beans
> Mixture of ½ cup sugar, ½ cup water, and ½ tea-spoon salt
> Later 1 teaspoon *shoyu*

Preparation: First soak the beans in three cups of water overnight. Then boil them until they soften. Put ½ cup of water, the sugar, and the salt into a saucepan and boil until the sugar is dissolved.

Add the beans and boil them for about 15 minutes

over a low flame. Allow them to simmer, then to cool. Leave them in the saucepan for another night to permit the sweetened water to soak into the beans. Next morning add a teaspoon of *shoyu* and boil the beans until all the water has evaporated. Serve in small individual bowls.

Skewered Fish

These are the special small fish one sees at the New Year's season. You may not like them much but try them once. You might easily be surprised.

Ingredients: 12 skewers of small silvery fish, *wakasagi* as they are known to the Japanese

A sauce of 1 tablespoon sugar, 3 tablespoons *shoyu*, and 1 tablespoon *sake*

Preparation: The small fish, easily obtained locally, should be spitted, broiled and served after repeated dippings in the sauce suggested. This is similar to the treatment of the chicken, the eel, and the shellfish chunks in an earlier chapter.

155

Girls have their traditional holiday on March 3, and of course, some ceremonial foods are habitually prepared for that occasion. These, however, do not properly fall under the heading of recipes that would be of interest to foreign cooks, with the exception of three that seem so unusual and delicious as to warrant inclusion at this point.

Shrimp and *Sake*

Shrimp come into their own again, for ladies only this time and young ladies at that.

Ingredients:
- 32 tiny shrimp
- 8 bamboo skewers
- 6 tablespoons *mirin*
- 8 tablespoons *shoyu*
- 2 1/2 tablespoons granulated white sugar

Preparation: Four shrimp at a time are skewered on each spit. Mix the *shoyu*, *mirin*, and sugar, and boil down. Broil the shrimp, soaking them in the mixture. Repeat twice. Serve individually.

Special Tangerine

This is a rare way of serving a delicious fruit.

Ingredients: 4 tangerines
4 sheets gelatin
1 cup water
¼ cup sugar

Preparation: Each tangerine is cut into a small basket shape. Make two halfway vertical cuts just away from the center, in the top one-third of the fruit. Make two other cuts horizontally, also halfway from each side, left to center and right to center. Take away the cut-away portions, plus the fleshy part of the fruit. Only the peeling thus remains and this forms a small-handled basket.

Melt the gelatin and add the sugar. Mix it with the fruit juice from the fruit portions that have been removed. When this mixture congeals put it back into the fruit skin.

Plum Blossom Egg

As colorful as a *kimono* wrapped in an *obi* and a lot tastier is this dish, a favorite of these young holiday-making girls.

Ingredients: 4 eggs
3 ½ tablespoons sugar
½ teaspoon salt

Some pinkish coloring
matter

Preparation: Break and beat the eggs,
add the salt, the sugar, and the pink coloring matter. Mix
thoroughly and boil lightly. The resultant mass may be
pressed with a special cutting tool that resembles a plum
or a cherry blossom, favorite flowers of all young girls.
The plum blossom shapes are eaten with joy and plea-
sure.

16

TABLE UTENSILS

Western-style equipment is more than adequate, but since this book deals with Japanese recipes and foodstuffs, it would seem wise to mention briefly the various types of Japanese kitchen equipment.

Legend suggests that the Japanese, ever close to nature, relied once on leaves for plates and twigs for chopsticks. Certainly today traces remain in the use of bamboo for chopsticks and, at the butcher shop, in the employment of the large bamboo leaf in which meat is wrapped.

Pottery plays a key role in Japan, shown artistically at the table in a wide variety of forms, shapes, and sizes and divided into many distinctive kinds, from the hard, white porcelain ware to the soft, dull-glazed folk pottery.

Japanese, whether using warm, earthenware utensils or gleaming, brightly-polished red, black, and gold lacquerware, always strive for harmony and identity

159

with nature, in the kitchen no less than before the guest.

The average household has the following utensils: rice bowls; soup bowls; large and medium dishes for food-serving; small dishes; saucers; chinaware plates and platters; handle-less teacups for Japanese tea; cups with handles and saucers for Western tea and coffee; dishes for fruit and cakes; and a wide range of chopsticks, from wood to bone, to ivory, to lacquer; and chopstick rests, also of various materials, in the shapes of reclining animals, leaves, twigs, pinecones, boats, fish, etc.

In the home one finds the separated chopsticks that the Japanese call *hashi;* in the restaurants, one finds the half-split type that are known as *waribashi,* used once, then thrown away.

Kitchen utensils follow Western pattern with a variety of knives, skillets, pans, pots, pitchers, teacups, pails, colanders, graters, ladles, sieves, cutting boards, cleavers, and the like, but there are also articles of distinctive Japanese origin:

There is the tub for the rice; the long slender knives used in preparing the filets of raw fish; the pestle for pounding the famous New Year's rice cakes; the wooden spatula for ladling the rice; the long iron

chopsticks for handling hot things; the bamboo
lattice mat for moulding the various kinds of *sushi*, or
rice-sandwiches; the sieve made from wood and horse-
hair; and the bamboo basket for use in straining and
draining vegetables.

TABLE MANNERS

This chapter will acquaint the foreigner with some of the simpler Japanese table etiquette, suggestions which will help avoid confusion and social error.

It starts quite simply with the single word, "*itadaki-masu*," literally meaning, "Now, I shall eat."

A small bow accompanies this remark and the host or hostess will respond with a small bow and say, "*Dozo*," or, "Please, go ahead."

Now a few good-natured hints.

First of all remove the cover from the individual rice bowl, a sign that shows Japan's staple food is being honored. Take the lid off with the left hand, and place it to one's left.

When rice is served, take up the bowl with both hands and place it on the extended tray. One hand is never used.

Always take the filled bowl and put it back on one's tray, and never start to eat directly upon receiving the filled bowl.

The chopsticks are picked up with the right hand and arranged for comfortable use with the left.

Soup, which takes much skill in making, should always be praised.

Do not eat the rice all at once. Return to it after tasting the other dishes.

Never eat pickles early in the dinner. Always save them for the last.

Never pour soup or any liquid other than tea over the rice, except in less formal dinners when this foreign habit may be excusable.

If one wishes more rice, leave a small mouthful in the bowl.

Rice when taken must all be eaten. Chinese and Japanese believe that any grain remaining will be a wart on a loved one's face. Rice left over implies waste, and waste is unforgivable in the often-hungry East.

An empty bowl signifies that a guest is finished and ready for the tea, which is sometimes poured into the same bowl.

Reverse the tips of the chopsticks before one helps himself to any community dish.

Before eating pickles one should rinse the ends of the used chopsticks in hot water.

Chopsticks themselves, when not in use, are returned to the right side of the tray. When the dinner is over, lay them on the tray itself, parallel to and in front of you and an inch or so apart.

Thanks for the repast should consist of the time-honored, " *Gochiso-sama deshita*," this meaning, "this has been a delicious dinner," or the simpler, "*Arigato gozaimashita*," or "thank you very much indeed."

In general, Japanese eat hot dishes first.

Care must be taken in removing lids from bowls. Easily wedged on, they are hard to remove without danger of spilling.

Replace all lids to all bowls at the conclusion of a dinner.

When chopsticks are used, insert them in the paper envelope in which they were first tendered after using.

When no more *sake* is desired, simply turn the small cup upside down.

Rice wine cups, even beer glasses, are often exchanged between guests and especially between guest and host. This may not appeal to foreigners even though a large bowl of hot water for rinsing the cup is usually present on the table, but it is best at least to know about this custom.

Here too are a few don'ts to tuck away for future reference.

Don't ask for knives, they are never served. This would imply the food is so tough it can't properly be eaten without them.

Don't pick up chopsticks until the older people present have first done so.

Don't scrape rice grains from chopsticks.

Don't take food from the soup before first raising the bowl.

Don't take right-side dishes with the left hand, or vice-versa.